MW01292038

I would like to dedicate this autobiography to my dear family for all their love and support, and their unyielding patience at times when I vented my frustrations in writing this book. They have given me more pleasure than I ever thought possible.

Printed: 2018

Cover Design: By Shandon Guthrie

WE WERE

We were before television,

Before penicillin, polio shots, antibiotics.

Before frozen foods, nylon, Xerox.

We were before radar, credit cards,

And ball point pens. For us,

Time sharing meant togetherness,

A chip meant a piece of wood,

Not part of a computer,

Hardware meant hardware,

Software wasn't even a word.

In those days, bunnies were

Small rabbits, and rabbits

Were not Volkswagons.

We were before Batman, Rudolph

The red nosed reindeer.

Before vitamin pills, disposable diapers,

Before scotch tape, M&M's, the automatic shift.

When we were young pizzas, cheerios, instant coffee, and McDonalds

Were unheard of. We thought fast food

Was what you ate during Lent.

We were before the FM radio,

Tape recorders, electric typewriters,

Word processors, electric music and disco dancing.

We were before pantyhose, and drip dry clothes.

Before ice makers and dishwashers, clothes dryers,

Freezers and electric blankets.

We got married first and then lived together.

In our day, cigarette smoking

Was fashionable, grass was mowed,

Coke was something you drank, and pot

Was something you cooked in.

We were before coin vending machines,

Jet planes, helicopters.

In our day, "Made in Japan" meant junk,

And the term "making out" referred to how you did on an exam.

In our time, there were 5 and 10 cent stores

Where you could buy things for 5 and 10 cents.

You could buy a new Chevy Coupe for $600,

But who could afford it in 1935.

Nobody. A pity, too,

Because gas was 11 cents a gallon.

We were not before the difference between the sexes

Was discovered, but we were before sex changes.

We just made do with what we had. And, so it was.

Author unknown

Preface

Most of us think we have at least one life story to tell, even, if just for our own families, this is my life story that all began almost eighty five years ago when I was born into a family of eleven children, on a farm in a remote area of a farming community with hard working, resilient people, that faced brutal challenges, where most knew of no other life but to follow in the tradition of their forefathers before them, from generation to generation, raising large families, toiling under the most harshest of conditions, day in and day out, week after week, year after year, just to survive on bare necessities.

All the years of my youth, which should have been the best years of my life, were instead hard, trying years; but as difficult as those years were, I feel somewhat privileged to have had the opportunity to be able to witness so much of today's modern technology that has evolved in the short span of my 85 years, of which I'm able to enjoy today. Like the fancy automobiles of today, as a child, the only transportation I knew was riding in a buggy or a wagon, hitched to a team of horses, trotting along a gravel road, where in the wintertime, we were being dragged through the snow banks, on a sleigh, filled with straw to sit on and wrapped in blankets to stay warm. I can still remember the thrill of my first ride in one of Henry Ford's new invention of the model T automobile, and very surprised to be moving down the road and not seeing the backside of a horse. I was already a teenager when I had my first experience of turning on a faucet over a sink, watching in disbelief when I saw water come pouring out without any effort to have to pump it from the well first. But nothing surprised me more until I saw a man walk on the moon and talk back to people here on earth, when I had always thought that the moon was nothing but a big ball of cheese. Then came the computer age, which I haven't quite conquered yet. The world seems like an open book from what I'm used to.

This is the legacy I wish to leave my children. I have had the support of my siblings, who helped refresh my memory when I had a senior moment. I will be referring to some of them throughout this book, so for that reason I will list them by name in the order we were born.

The eldest, Theodore (Ted) was born August 4, 1916. We lost this beloved brother, a few years back, at the age of 86.

Leonard was born November 2, 1918. Leonard died at the age of 92.

Esther, the first girl, was born September 20, 1920. She recently died at the age of 91.

Dorothea was born April 21, 1922. She died at the age of 87.

Martha, born April 20, 1924, is currently 88 years old.

Arthur (Art) was born March 26, 1926. He died at the age of 85.

Etta (myself) was born May 2, 1928.

Hildegard was born April 30, 1930

Ella was born November 2, 1934.

Clifford, born April 26, 1936, died too soon at 75 years old.

Betty, the baby, was born June 11, 1938.

My Parents Wedding Picture

Family Picture Taken In 1941

Family Picture taken in 1991, Fifty Years Later

CHAPTER 1

Living out in the country meant a long drive to town, a long drive to church, a long walk to the little red school house, which was some two miles away and was a typical country one room school house, consisting of a total of 20 to 25 school children, with just the one teacher to teach all eight grades, where the grades were merely separated by a desk. Just making it to school every morning was a major undertaking most of the time.

When I was eleven years old, I became the oldest of three of us children going to school, the older siblings by now having completed eighth grade. I was made responsible for my two younger sisters, Hildegard age 9 and Ella age 6, to get us safely to school every morning. I already had the experience from my older siblings, that if we walked kitty-corner across our neighbors farmland, it would cut down the walking distance considerably, but it was a route that made it necessary for us to have to climb over or duck under several barbed wire fences along the way. So we stomped through the muddy and dirty fields, out in nowhere, where all you could see was a barn off in the distance and a few animals grazing nearby. We started off to school one morning, what I thought was a normal morning, which turned out not to be such a normal morning. As we started to walk and approached the first fence to crawl under and we saw this huge red curly haired bull standing on the other side of the fence, looking as surprised to see us as we were to see him. We had never seen this bull before, so I assumed that our farmer neighbor had recently acquired him. He looked very frightening, having a humped back, resembling a buffalo, he had this huge brass ring hanging from his nose. Now, we were used to all sorts of animals on our farm, but this strange bull looked down right frightening and mean, so I was afraid to cross over that fence with my two little sisters. We turned to walk back home, then noticed the bull slowly wander away, we waited till we felt safe, then we crossed over the fence and took off running for the next fence, but as soon as the bull spotted us running, he came trotting back toward us, so we only made it as far as a rock pile, (more on rock piles later in the book). We climbed to the top of this rock pile and watched the bull standing there, kicking up dirt with his hoofs, which I had always thought was an indication that they were mad. We waited till he slowly lumbered away, then we held each other's hands and ran for the next nearest fence, crawled under to safety and made it to school, all be it, late!! I still can't explain why I never told the teacher about this nor did I tell my parents about it after school. With so many children, I guess we were to be seen and not heard. This bull continued to prowl those pastures, but he only seemed to be there in the mornings, we never saw him there coming home from school. This became an every morning ritual. So we developed a pattern, running from fence to rock pile, then rock pile to fence again, we were becoming fairly good at estimating our safest distance, UNTIL... this one morning, I obviously misjudged his distance or else I got braver, but as we were running for the last fence, this bull was nipping at our heels, I was dragging Ella through the dirt and we made it through to the other side of the fence by a nose, the bull's nose. Then Ella started to cry, telling me that I had ruined her little red coat that mother had her wear that morning, that's when I saw a red flag go up, "RED COAT!!" thinking that was not a good idea! I decided it was time to talk to mother about this, no more red coats. I approached her that evening and vented my frustrations about this whole scenario we faced every single morning. She already knew that the neighbor had a new bull, but she knew nothing of these struggles we faced every morning. She calmly listened to me and when I was finished she calmly said to me "If that bull ever gets too close to you, you need to pull hard on that brass ring on his nose, that's what it is there for, it will hurt him bad and he'll leave you alone". End of discussion!! I shrugged my shoulders and walked away not being too happy with her solution, my common sense told me that I never wanted to get that close, but in the back of my mind there was always this inkling, that at least I had an option. It was the only sound advice I had been given thus far. So off to school we went as usual, no more questions asked, but the bull fight went on till winter set in when he suddenly disappeared and I never saw him again. I always hoped that the farmer had sold him, or perhaps butchered him for some tough steaks.

CHAPTER 2

This all started with the arranged marriage of my parents, on October 15, 1915, when my mother was given a dowry (wedding gift) of a 800 acre farm from her father on her wedding day. This farm was located among a wide array of similar farms in the area of the city of Hague, No Dakota. The house that came with this farm is where my parents started their life together, and where they would have a total of eleven children, all born at home, with the sole assistance of just a midwife, who ultimately delivered each one of us, a healthy, hearty, robust child, a blessing for the tough road that awaited us. When mother became pregnant with her second child, this one room house, which had served them as their kitchen, living room, bedroom, was now getting a bit crowded. So dad got busy and build a new one bedroom house, which had a narrow stairway, that led up to an unfinished attic, which ultimately became the sleeping quarters for all eleven of us children, sometimes, 3 or 4 to a bed. This attic was never completely finished, where rafters were left exposed. It was just one room that had a small window at either end, with a kerosene lamp sitting on a dresser for lighting. The boys slept on one end of this room, the girls slept on the other end of the room. The roof came to a point in the center of this room then sharply slanted down the sides, where you could only stand up straight in the center of the room which made it so our faces were very close to the roof edge when we were lying in bed. In the wintertime, it got so cold in that attic, that the frost on the windows, was as thick on the inside as it was on the outside, and the only heat we ever got up there, was what little wafted up through a small grate like opening, located on the floor, directly over the pot-bellied coal stove in the living room below. Having no indoor plumping, and needing to walk to the outhouse in the pitch dark of night, in those cold winters, where temperatures dropped as low as 40 degrees below zero, with snow up to your hips, made it necessary for us to have cans of pee under our beds, instead of canopies over our beds

The positive side to all this was, our parents made sure that we were always warm and cozy under wool and goose down comforters and pillows, but they didn't come easy.

Dad raised his own sheep, which he would shear every year and we loved watching him desperately hold on to this struggling sheep while he was shearing away, clear to the naked skin. Then he would bring all of this dirty, bloody, stinky wool, into our kitchen where we'd spent many evenings sitting around, processing this wool. Dad would strap about a 6" square wooden block on our hands, where the underside of this block was covered with hundreds of little sharp needles. We would each take a hunk of this newly sheared wool, then we would twist and pull that piece between those sharp needles, till it became a nice clean, fluffy, piece of wool, which we would then throw into a bin until all the wool was clean. Then mother would make us nice thick wool comforters that no amount of cold could penetrate. There was no doubt that we got a lot of satisfaction in being so cozy warm, because we knew where they came from.

All our pillows were equally as plush and just as hard to come by. Mother took great pride in the flock of geese she was raising on the farm, mainly for their down. She took such pride on plucking days, where she would set up her station, outside in the yard, where she would be sitting on a chair and have us younger children round up the geese, and bring them to her one at a time. She had furnished us with a very long stick that had a wire hook on one end with which we would snag the goose by the leg and reel him in. We would then pick it up and carry it to mother's station, while we were franticly trying to hang on to this very excited goose, flapping his wings against every part of our bodies, giving us a beating that I don't think even Joe Louis got jabs like that. Many times they'd flap right out of our hands, and we'd have to go chase after it again. After we brought the goose to mother, she would grab this struggling goose with complete ease, then she would flip him upside down onto her lap and immediately pinch their long necks between her knees, then with perfect speed and precision, she would begin to pluck their soft, snow white down from their undersides, all the while this goose is loudly squawking and furiously pecking at mother's legs until they would bleed, and yet, mother had a continues smile on her face, I don't know if it was because she enjoyed it so much, or if it was the satisfaction of "I gotcha where I want you." By the end of the day, the bins were running over with snow white fluffy down for our new pillows, but we had gashes and black blue marks, which mother would treat with liniment and iodine. If there was a good goose down crop, mother would also make goose down comforters for all of us. On the other hand, the mattresses we slept on were not so plush. Those were made with a very heavy canvas which was stuffed with new straw that would poke through the canvas when we laid on it, and if that didn't keep you awake, the rustling noise they made, did every time someone moved, and with four to a bed, someone was always moving.

CHAPTER 3

The winters were spent keeping warm, and the summers were spent staying safe, where the winter blizzards were horrible, and the summer storms were horrendous.

Our refuge during some of these big storms took place in what we called "the cellar". It was simply a big unfinished dirt hole under our house. The floor door in our pantry in the kitchen was the only access we had to this cellar under the house. Mother also used this floor door, for storage and it was always loaded with stuff. So when we were warned of an oncoming storm, that floor was cleaned off faster than the lighting that was coming. There were just three little steps leading down to the cellar where the walls were just fresh black dirt, the floor was also plain black dirt, it looked as though it had just been freshly dug. All you could see when you were down there, was the underside of the house, and that was only if mother had time to grab a kerosene lamp for light, otherwise, it was pitch dark down there. There was a narrow bench, on which mother would sit, as we all huddled around her like a mother hen with her brood of baby chicks, as the storm was raging on, we all stayed perfectly quiet, as the house above us would shake and crackle as if it was going to fly off its foundation any minute. It certainly put the fear of God in us, so much so, that I still fear a thunderstorm today. When everything was finally quiet, dad would climb out and sneak a peek, making sure that all was clear and safe for us to scramble back to civilization. There was another backup cellar outside on the grounds, away from the house, for anyone that might be working or playing outside and didn't have enough time to make it to the house before the storm hit. The outside cellar was a cave like hole, in the ground, with an old dilapidated wood door lying over a mound of dirt on the top of this cellar. Again we would be sitting on a dirt floor, till we saw the sun peeking through all the cracks on the door above us, before we could come crawling out, hoping that everyone in the other cellar was safe. Dad would be looking around as if he were counting us. All this had to have been some very traumatic moments for my parents, trying to keep us safe. Considering some of the horrible losses that some of our neighbor farmers experienced from some of these storms, we were very lucky most of the time. We only lost one of our storage sheds, when this big black funnel of a tornado suddenly appeared in the sky, and very quickly came sweeping through our farm, picking up one of our sheds and twisting it into a thousand pieces in seconds, then the funnel would disappear as fast as it appeared, while we were all watching in horror. There was always clean-up day after every storm, and this particular one was huge.

The one thing that always puzzled me, was, why our outhouse was never properly anchored down. Without fail, and with every storm that came along, the outhouse had toppled over and had rolled away, lying around the farm somewhere. The boys would then go get it, carry it back to its original location, then simply plop it over its hole again. It's a good thing we all knew the exact spot where it was located at all times, because if it wasn't there, you can be sure we stayed clear from that location. During those dark nights, we would flash around our flashlights a plenty, with every step we took. If that outhouse happened to be occupied when the wind began to blow, you can be sure to see someone running from it with their trousers wrapped around their knees. With the summer storms now over, we got ready for the winter blizzards.

Walking to school was a must, unless, it became next to impossible, and many times this was the case. There were days where we would sink into the snow, up to our hips with every step we took till we could stomp no more, before dad would come to our rescue, using the box like sled which he had built. It was just that, a large square wood box, which he had equipped with ski runners for the winter, and could be converted to wheels for other uses. He built two rails to which he would hitch one of our horses, we called Tom. He put wing like boards which protruded out each side of the box, which prevented this sled from toppling completely over.

There were two small benches inside and straw on the floor. The benches were useless, most of the time we were tumbling all over each other, onto the straw floor, as we were being dragged over hill and dale, climbing over snow drift after snow drift as high as a house. Dad would sit there flapping the reins, that he had pulled through a small hole he had cut through the front for a window and he repeatedly said, "Giddy up, Giddy up" when it looked like old Tom couldn't giddy up another step. It was sad to watch this poor horse use every muscle in his body, which was by now covered with white ice crystals, as if his sweat was freezing as fast as he was sweating, all the while the snow was coming down hard, and visibility was next to none, there were no trails or roads to follow, no barbed wire fences to cross, they were all buried in the snow, just blankets of white snow as far as the eye could see. Dad would just head in the direction of the school, sitting in front of this little open window, icicles hanging from his nose (I wonder what that was). This was a ride you couldn't find, even at Disneyland. At the end of the school day, dad would go through this same routine to come back to pick us up again. Being late for school on those kinds of days, were all but ignored.

There was one other morning as we were walking to school which we didn't soon forget. There were four of us, Martha, Arthur, Myself, &Hildegard, starting off for school with just a few snow flurries beginning to come down, but as storms sometimes do, they can quickly turn into a full blown blizzard in minutes, that morning it did just that. We were soon walking in a blizzard that became so blinding we soon lost all sense of direction. Martha and Art were soon in a heated discussion on the proper direction to the school. Martha being sure of the direction she thought we should be going, while Art was sure of another direction, Martha finally took a hold of mine & Hildegard's hand and proceeded walking in the direction where she thought the school would be, while Art stubbornly took off the other direction he was sure of. It turned out that Martha had been right and the three of us, groping through this blinding blizzard, finally walked right up to this school, half frozen but alive. Art was nowhere to be seen. I don't' recall if we even mentioned anything to the teacher about Art being lost alone out there in that awful blizzard, but I know that nobody went looking for him. Finally, very late in the day, Art walked into the school, looking like one big icicle; his eyes were blood red, looking as if he might have been crying. He had been walking in that blizzard all day looking for the school. The teacher allowed him to sit by the potbellied coal stove for the rest of the day, which was by now nearly over. The blizzard had let up considerably by now, so we all walked home together after school. Those guardian angels were hard at work that day. I don't recall even mentioning any of this to our parents after school, we were home safe and that's all that mattered, just another hurdle that we conquered.

One early fall, our brother Art, came up with an idea that would get us to school without having to walk all the time. He decided to build a cart to which he could hitch our Shetland pony and have him pull us to school in it. This project turned into a catastrophe, before it barely got off the ground. He built this small simple cart, using materials lying around the farm, which dad allowed him to use. This cart had three sides, leaving it open across the back in order to fit all five of us that were now going to school, so some of us could dangle our feet across this open back. The five of us were Martha, Arthur, Myself, Hildegard, & Ella. As he was building this cart, mistake number one might have been that he equipped it with two oversized buggy wheels with wooden spokes he found lying around the farm. The first day it was ready for us to ride to school, we started out like gangbusters as we all happily piled in, Art throwing on a bag of hay for the pony that day who we left in the little barn next to the schoolhouse. Off we went screaming with joy at this wonderful experience, too good to be true, as it eventually turned out to be. We were now required to take the route of the gravel highway, clippity clop, clippity clop on this noisy gravel highway, as we neared the school, all the children, including the teacher, were standing outside the school watching as we approached waving and screaming as if we were celebrities. It was the most exhilarating experience that was well worth the woes that awaited us. Less than a week later, we piled in, feeling as though we had conquered the world, our parents were standing there looking at us with this puzzled look on their faces, we all waved as we pulled away and went clippity clop down the road, until about half way to school, we were traveling down the usual slope going at a pretty good pace, when, in a split second, this pony suddenly whipped us off the main highway, following a newly made wagon trail into a farmer's field, crossed over a deep borrow pit which caused our cart to break up into pieces, scattering us all over that field, wooden wheel spokes raining on us. We all got ourselves up, brushing clumps of dirt off our clothes, no one was hurt, thank God, so we all got busy hunting down our books strewn all over the field, we gathered what lunch we could still salvage, then we walked the rest of the way to school while Art rode the pony to school. At the end of the day, walking home from school, Art asked if we would stop at the scene of the accident and carry home any pieces that could still be salvaged, he was determined to rebuild this cart again. So now were carrying home armloads of pieces from this cart, Art did get busy rebuilding it, but this time he equipped it with metal wheels. As soon as he had rebuilt it, we got ready to take it to school again, but the first time, as a precaution, Art got off the cart at this crucial point where the pony seemed to have a fetish about. Even at that, that pony nearly pushed Art into the borrow pit when we reached that trail, Art kept him under control and we got passed it just fine, so that's what we did for about a week, when Art decided to give it another try, and we took off one morning, going down the same little slope, trotting right along, and sure enough, we came to that trail and the pony did a complete rerun, whipping us all over the field again the cart falling to pieces. We picked ourselves up again and told Art we'd had enough of his bright idea as he rode off on his pony to school and we walked from then on, no more bright ideas.

CHAPTER 4

I'm still in awe of the kind of superwoman our
mother must have been, keeping up with all she
was required to do, day in and day out, under the
most harshest of circumstances and conditions,
most of the time. I never saw her sit down and
relax, or read a book, and I'm not even sure she
ever got a good night's rest, mainly because; she
always had a new baby to tend to. If my math is
correct, in order to bear eleven children, one every
two years, she would have had to been pregnant
most of her adult life and at the same time also
have a toddler to run after.

She was always in the kitchen, cooking and baking,
on an old wood burning stove that needed constant
stoking with anything that would burn, and had an
ashcan that needed to be emptied every so often.
There was no temperature control on the oven, yet,
she regularly baked a dozen loaves of bread, three
times a week, which came out of that oven a
perfect golden brown, every single time, and
absolutely delicious. There was not one modern
convenience available for her to work with. There
were no cabinets, no sinks, no shelves; all of her

work was all done on the kitchen table, where we ate all our meals. This was a long table, a bench along each side, where all us children would be seated, there was a chair on either end where mom and dad would sit, nicely situated, where they could still reach across the table and whack any of us over the head, if we didn't behave. The few plates and cups we had were in a free standing cupboard, that had a narrow shelf across the front, on which sat an ever present galvanized bucket, filled with fresh well water and holding an enamel dipper to use for anyone that needed a drink. We would simply fill this dipper with water, then drink what we wanted of it, then we would plop the dipper back into the bucket, leftovers and all, if there was any. Next to this bucket sat a small enamel basin and a bar of soap with which to wash our hands, after which we had to pick up the basin with this now dirty water, open the screen door and swoosh it outside onto the ground. If someone happened to be coming around the corner at that particular moment, so be it!!

Our lifeline and sole source of water came from the windmill that stood among the many buildings on our farm. It would supply all of our water needs, as long as the wind was blowing strong enough to blow the big wheel around to operate the pump, but many times, when the wind wasn't blowing, it became necessary for us to convert the pump to it's manual position, so we were able to pump the water manually which was a job that was normally given to us younger ones, so young, that there were times when it took two of us to hang on to the long pump handle to bring it up and down to pump the water. We were given shiny new galvanized buckets, with which to carry the water from one place to another, wherever needed, and it was always needed somewhere. We needed to carry every drop of this water to the house for all its needs; we had to carry it to all the water troughs throughout the farm for the smaller animals to drink from. The larger livestock drank from a huge tank that butted up to the windmill pump, which had to be pumped full of water at all times. Amazingly, this tank had been built on a slang, where in the summertime, we had to pump and pump till this tank overflowed where the water would slush over its sides and trickle down a rocky slope into the vegetable garden nearby. What the water didn't reach, we had to carry in buckets to finish watering the garden. These were ongoing chores that went year in and year out; it became brutal in the wintertime, where de-icing became very difficult at times when the troughs would freeze up and we had to chip the ice loose. When the winds became too strong or in the case of a coming storm, we had to shut down the windmill wheel by pulling on a lever and securing it tightly so the wheel would fold up and unable to fly around and possibly cause serious damage. This became a regular evening ritual in case of a surprise storm, but had to be opened up again every morning. Even today, when I see people ooh and aah over a beautiful windmill, it still looks like a lot of work to me.

CHAPTER 5

Another ongoing chore was milking all of the cows every morning and every evening, that was a must. By milking time, their udders would be so swollen with milk they could hardly walk. First we had to go to the meadows and round them up, then lead them to the barn, and place them in their proper stalls. Everyone had to do their fair share of milking as soon as we were old enough to learn. When my turn came, dad had a problem! There is a trick to squeezing those "tits" just right to have the milk come spurting out, I could never get the hang of it when my turn came, every cow dad gave me to milk kicked me out from under her and I would go flying, bucket with a few drops of milk and all. Dad finally told me not to milk anymore, saying that I was wasting too much milk. I thought I guess it doesn't matter that I might get seriously hurt, only that I was wasting too much milk. It was just as well because now I could stand on the sidelines with the other kids and have our sisters, who always did the milking, spray milk straight from the udder at our wide open mouths, but all we usually got was a face full of warm milk. After milking was completed, the buckets of milk were carried to what we called the summer kitchen (the little house mom and dad had lived in before the new house was built) there we had a milk separator where we would pour the milk into a large stainless steel tub, sitting on top of this separator, then we would turn the handle and see sweet cream come pouring out one spout and skim milk pouring out of the second spout. Mother would then hold back what she needed for household use, dad always sold the sweet cream but all the skim milk was fed to the baby calves that were already lined up outside, their tails wagging, waiting for their milk. We would put a serving of skim milk in a bucket which we would hold up for them to drink from, they would drink so heftily that we could hardly hang on to the bucket. There were so many calves we would slap a glob of milk foam on their backs as we fed them which left a wet spot so we could tell which calf had already had their milk, so they wouldn't get it a second time or maybe even none at all. Mom always had a pitcher of raw milk on the dinner table. There was never a shortage of dairy products for mother's use in the kitchen. She would make all of her own cottage cheese, yogurts, butter, where us kids would have to stand by a churner and spent hours pushing the butter stick up and down, till grains of butter started to float in the buttermilk. She would then mold the butter into a ball and make delicious dishes with the leftover buttermilk. Nary had a speck ever gone to waste. I am still puzzled, that with such an abundance of butter and eggs, why we never once got buttered toast or eggs for breakfast. As a matter of fact, I never knew that eggs are actually a breakfast item, till many years later. Mother always insisted that we start breakfast with something warm in our tummies, so it was usually hot cooked cereals, such as oatmeal, cream of wheat, cracked or whole wheat, which we would fetch from our grain shed and grind ourselves, grasshopper legs and all. But on Sunday mornings we would get a treat of corn flakes or puffed wheat. But mother would heat a pot of milk on the stove and have us use hot milk on our cereals, which soaked up all the snap, crackle, and pop, that all the cereal companies are so proud of today. It was a habit I could never shake and I still need to use hot milk on my cereal. Try it, you might like it!!

We were always in awe, when we watched mother make meals from an array of dough she could put together. All of her dishes were so delicious; that I don't think even Emeril Lagasse could match today.

She always had an abundance of eggs, cream, milk, also sacks and sacks of white flour, which dad traded for wheat after every fall harvest. I suppose, that this was a big help during the depression years because we never went hungry. I remember how we used to be all eyes whenever we watched mother make her tubs of pastry dough which she would then roll out into paper thins sheets, getting them ready to dry where she would place two chairs back to back, outside in the yard directly in the sun. Then she would place toweled pillows across the chair backs and drape her sheets of dough over the top. She would have us kids stand there for hours waving white towels to keep away any flies that attempted to land on her dough. Believe me, nary a fly ever got a mouth full. When the dough was ready, mother would roll it into cylinders, then with a very sharp knife and with perfect precision and speed, she would cut her noodles in sizes and widths of her choice. We would cringe watching the rhythm of the knife's edge coming dangerously close to her fingers. When dinner was served we would climb into our assigned seats at the table, each of us would say our short prayer, and before the last amen was said, there were a hundred hands reaching for food.

The one that ate the fastest got the mostest. Maybe that accounts for the reason that I am still a fast eater today. Us sisters are still sorry, that we failed to get some of mother's recipes when we had the chance. We've all tried to duplicate some of them, without much luck. I suppose they will remain secret recipes forever. I don't mean to insinuate that all of our meals were from pastry dough, we always had a big variety of meats and vegetables also, all of what we raised and grew on the farm ourselves. (More on that later in the book.) All the food we consumed, came from farm to table, everything was homegrown, from meat to vegetables to desserts, even snacks like popcorn, sunflower seeds and more. Pesticides were unheard of, there might have been a bug here or there, but what you don't know don't hurt you.

CHAPTER 6

The necessities of everyday life became major
productions. Like our bath nights that took place
every Saturday night, and the only day we got to
bathe. This took place in the summer kitchen,
where we had an old fashioned bathtub with its
drain sitting over a small hole in the wood floor,
through which the dirty water would flow under the
house. Hildegard and I would have to spend all day
every Saturday heating the water in boiler pots on
top of an old wood burning stove which we stoked
with anything we could find that would burn. The
water needed to be brought to a full boil so mother
could dilute it with cold water in order to have
enough to go around, even at that, more than one
of us were bathed in the same water, then it would
be drained for the next batch of kids. Sometimes
Hildegard and I would get so bored heating water
all day that we would run to the chicken coop, get
some eggs, and boil them in old rusty cans we'd find
laying around, then eat boiled eggs all day. That
was a secret we had to keep or we'd have had a line
of kids waiting for boiled eggs.

After dinner on Saturday night we would take our pajamas and run to the summer kitchen, get bathed, put on our pajamas, and run back to the house and promptly go to bed. The older ones bathed later, always leaving mom and dad for last. Running back to the house in the wintertime was a chilly experience. There were no robes for any of us, as soon as we got up in the mornings we would slip on our bib overalls for the day, whether it was for work or school. Come Sunday morning, we were sparkling clean for church and a day of rest, where we were not allowed to do any kind of unnecessary work, unless a cow fell in the well, luckily, that never happened. Before church, the cows had to be milked and all the necessary chores had to be completed, then breakfast and dressing up in our fineries, all the while, dad was all dressed up in his suit and Sunday hat, sitting in the car, honking the horn for mother to hurry up. We would all pack into our two-door model A- Ford, like sardines are packed in a can, with mom and dad in the front seat, with an ever present baby on mother's lap, the rest of us crowded in the back seat, sitting double layer on each others laps.

When weather permitted, dad would take a short cut through neighbor's farmland, on a ruddy, bumpy, two lane road, as we were jostled around, till we were dizzy. Dad had to stop at several stiles (cattle openings) on the way, where one of the boys then had to crawl all over us to get out of the car, and open those stiles. Dad would then drive through, the stiles would be closed again, and our brother came climbing all over us again. I hope mother didn't iron our clothes, because it wouldn't have mattered in the end. But it was truly a welcoming sight as we arrived at the little white church, with its lovely steeple sticking up, as if to welcome us. We entered the church through two huge mahogany doors to a beautiful sight of scarlet red carpet, lined with rows of mahogany pews; very striking indeed. But for whatever reason, families never sat together. The men were always seated on one side, while all the women wearing their big hats, and were seated on the other side of the aisle. The children were all seated at the very front of the church, not for Sunday school, but where the elders of the church would teach us how to read and write the German language, which we all successfully accomplished. Consequently, we couldn't speak a word of English when we started first grade, but luck was on our side, most of the teachers we had, had came from our same community and spoke fluent German themselves, so they were well qualified to deal with us and actually taught us the English language fairly fast. The church service was conducted in German, all of their literature was printed in German, and we always had to sit through the one hour German sermons, about all the hellfire and damnation that awaited us if we didn't behave, and behave we did, this burning in hell forever, didn't sound very pleasant. After chugging back home, the same way we came, we had to change from our fineries into our overalls again, then we would sit around the table for our every Sunday meal of mother's homemade chicken noodle soup, floating with yellow chicken and loaded with homemade noodles, there would also be a large bowl of a mixture of peanut butter and dark Karo syrup, a tub of homemade butter, all of which to slather on mother's homemade bread which was piled high on a large platter in front of us. After our meal and the dishes were washed, we were ordered to rest, like the good book says. Believe me, we welcomed and needed it. There was one Sunday, I didn't soon forget. We had just arrived home from church, and barely made it into the house, when the sky suddenly got very dark, the wind was starting to blow and it looked as if a surprise storm was brewing. Before we had even changed our clothes, we were all looking out the window watching dad's beautiful wheat fields, tall and almost ready for harvest, swaying in the wind, looking a little like ocean waves, it was actually quite a beautiful sight to see. Suddenly, it began to rain harder and harder, which soon turned into a hailstorm, hail as large as golf balls. After this storm passed, this beautiful wheat field we had all admired just minutes before, had now been totally flattened, all you could see was clumps of twisted stalks lying everywhere. What haunted me for many years after was seeing dad still wearing his suit, pull up a chair, sit down, pull out a snow white hankie from his suit pocket, put it to his face and sob, uncontrollably, like I'd never seen anyone cry before or since. I can imagine what he must have felt at that moment, seeing the livelihood of his large family go down the drain in the twinkling of an eye. No time to replant, gone, kaput!!!!! I don't know the full outcome of it all, but what I do know, is that we kept on eating and staying warm.

CHAPTER 7

Getting the farm prepared for spring planting was a lot of work where we first had to clear acres and acres of all the debris it had collected during the winter months. Tumbleweeds were rampant everywhere, some were as big as a car but light as a feather. Dad would hand us each a pitchfork and a box of matches to the older boys; we gleaned the fields stacking tumbleweeds into one pile after another throughout the fields. Then one of the boys would light a match and throw it into each pile, "POOF" it went up like paper, piles of these very dry tumbleweeds burning everywhere, it looked like a war zone. We were then all given our area to cover, keeping them contained from spreading. In all the years we did this, there was never one accident, nor was there one tumbleweed ever left behind. We were a very responsible crew. As soon as the tumbleweeds had been all cleared off of the fields, we had to go back to these same fields and now clear them of stones and rocks of all sizes that seemed to come to the surface every spring. I still don't understand that phenomenon but they were there. To do this chore, we needed to take a team of horses hitched to a wagon and have them pull along side of us, as we stooped to pick up the rocks and hurl them up into this wagon. Some of those rocks were so large, that some of us younger ones needed help to lift them up into the wagon. Many of these rocks were deeply embedded in the soil which took a lot of kicking and twisting to loosen them up, very time consuming. The wagon full of rocks was then taken to a location on the farm, which might already have a formed rock pile from previous years, otherwise, we just started a new rock pile. Hence the rock piles I referred to, earlier in the book, what became our refuge from the bull. Everyday started with milking the cows and doing all the necessary chores each morning and each evening. At the end of the day there was no television, no reading books, no games to play, we just ate our dinner and went straight to bed dead tired.

Dad and the boys usually did all the planting of the crops, and it wasn't long before those fields sprouted into a sea of green fields which became an enticing sight for the livestock grazing nearby, which now made us cow herders, where we would have to go and sit in the meadows all day to keep the cattle from straying into these green wheat fields. If any one animal strayed, we had to run and turn them back into the meadows where they belonged. It was truly a boring job, but we made use of some of our time, catching gophers. There were so many gophers eating the crops that the agriculture department offered to pay a penny a tail for every gopher we caught, dad furnished us with plenty of traps and was always happy to see us catch as many gophers as we did. Besides trapping them we had another way to catch them. We would put a noose on one end of a long heavy string, which we then circled around the perimeter of the gopher hole, then we would very quietly sit back a ways and wait for the gopher to stick his head out of the hole, I suppose to see if the coast was clear, but they were usually badly mistaken, because we would yank the string at that point and noose them almost every time. At one time Hildegard and I each had a shoebox full of squirrel tails which we just pounded off the dead squirrel with a rock, on another rock. We kept them salted so they wouldn't spoil, till dad could take them to town to sell. We kept catching them and dad kept selling them but he never gave us the money.

CHAPTER 8

Working in dirty fields, all day long, our dirty overalls were piling up fast, and laundry day was only once a week. Another busy day for us, again took place in the summer kitchen where Hildegard and I were back to heating water in boiler pots and eating boiled eggs. Weather permitting, mother would sort all the dirty clothes, according to color and pile them around the ground outside. When she finished, there were so many piles it reminded me of the badlands in Montana. I was told, before I was born that mother was doing laundry in a tub using a washboard, but all I remember is an old wringer washing machine, that had a little gas motor sitting underneath it, it would shake and quiver and periodically would stop all together, then we would have to wait for it to cool off before it would start up again. One of us had to crank the wringer by hand, while another one of us would feed the clothes into it, and the clothes would then drop into a huge laundry basket sitting behind the washer. We would then carry them to the clotheslines, and with what seemed like a bushel of clothespins, we would hang rows and rows of wet clothes on these lines. In the wintertime, the clothes would freeze so stiff they would stick out as if we were still in them. When the time came to bring them into the house, we couldn't fit them through the door, many times we had to break them in half. Some needed to be laundered again due to all the birds that flew over them hanging on these clotheslines.

With mother's constant cooking and baking and constantly heating water, we used up a lot of fuel, so they would have us kids hunt for anything that would burn; sticks, twigs, corn husks, but most of all, dried manure. They would send us out to the meadows to scout for cow chips, we would turn over cow chips all day, then we had to leave them to dry on their bottom sides for a day. We then needed to go back and collect them the next day while flipping over any new ones to be collected the next day. This was an ongoing chore all summer, stacking them up for winter use. To break the monotony, we would have a contest to see which one of us could turn over the biggest cow chip without breaking it up. This was actually very difficult, because a lot of them were stuck to the grass underneath, but we took a lot of pride in winning. At the same time we also had to clean the stalls in the barn, shoveling manure into wheelbarrows then wheel it to a manure bed that had already been started next to the barn. We kept adding manure to that manure bed as it was drying and stomp it down with our feet till it was packed hard and dry. Then it would be cut into blocks and stacked along side the cow chips for winter fuel. I don't think my daughters could ever quite understand me, when I used to tell them that, "I've had to haul a lot of shit in my day!"

Anywhere we worked or played, livestock was always all around us, almost as if we were one of them. Some of my siblings even had their favorites and considered them their pets. Personally, I was never fond of any of them and they weren't too fond of me and. They always seemed to be picking on me, the cows kicked me, the chickens pecked me, the sheep butted me, the bull chased me, I couldn't even walk past a rooster where he didn't raise his big red comb, spread his wings, and come running after me. My siblings always told me that I was making the mistake by running away from them. But I couldn't see standing still where three geese at a time, would come running after me with their six foot wings spread and squawks that could be heard in China. One day, I happened to be at the far end of the farm, when this sheep buck, for whatever reason, began to chase after me. He ran so fast I could barely stay ahead of him, when I quickly decided to change course and head for the blacksmith shop where I knew dad would be working, as I flew by the shop, screaming, "Pawpa Pawpa" which means "Daddy Daddy" in German. I was so relieved to see him step outside the blacksmith only to hear him say, "Schpringe schpringe", which means "Run run" in German. At that moment all I could think of was what do you think I have been doing the last quarter mile, but I also knew that I was on my own now and I quickly found refuge in a crack between two buildings. There I waited him out until he slowly walked away. This was one mean buck, always chasing someone one time or another, one day this buck chased my sister Dorthea, she went running straight for the barn, screaming for her sister Martha to slide open the barn door. As soon as Martha did that, Dorthea ran into the barn and in a second she turned around in time to grab this big buck by the horns, then she yelled for Martha to pin his neck by closing the barn door. As soon as Martha closed the door on him, his head was now inside and his body was on the outside of the barn. Dorthea picked up a big stick

and ferociously beat this buck over his head. Then
she released him and the buck slowly staggered
away shaking his head.

CHAPTER 9

This was everyday life for us, we knew of no other, except, going to school and going to church every Sunday morning. We did get a wonderful treat once a year, where folks would take us to the annual 4th of July celebration in the small town of Hague. We really looked forward to this day, but there were consequences. Every year, just before the 4th, we were warned that every stitch of work on that farm had to be completed, before we were allowed to go to this celebration. I'm thinking that it was mostly a threat, because mom and dad never wanted to miss that day themselves. But still we hustled, day and night to make sure there was not one weed left in the garden, the house was spic and span everything was caught up. The morning of the 4th, we put on our fineries and dad would hand each of us a nickel to spend any way we wanted to. Wow!! So every year I was in a dilemma. Deciding whether to buy an ice cream cone or a cracker jack, they each cost a nickel. I would usually buy a cracker jack one year then an ice cream cone the next year. When temptation became too strong, we would trade a kernel of cracker jack for a lick of ice cream. Most of the day, us younger ones would usually huddle around mother, while dad was off somewhere doing his own thing. But as sure as the clock struck noon, he'd show up for a bologna sandwich which mother always brought along. I remember one year we had just finished our lunch, when this fellow was lining up all the 8 year olds for the foot race, although, I had no idea of what it was all about, when mother suddenly shoved me into this line up, I thought she was trying to get rid of me than I heard this gentleman say "GO" and mother yelled, "schpring schpring, Run Run", well I'd been chased by enough animals, I surely knew how to run. So I started to run, I kept on running until I reached the fence at the end of the line, when I stopped, this short stocky fellow, wearing a suit, black bow tie, and a black derby hat, reached out with his cane, he was carrying, he hooked it around my arm and pulled me towards him. I got so frightened. I thought that my mother had sold me. Then the man handed me a fifty cent piece for winning first place in the race, but that didn't excite me nearly as much as it did when he turned me loose to run back to my mama. She took the fifty cent piece from me and we all got both the ice cream cone and a cracker jack that year. No one patted me on the back for a job well done; they were all too busy scarfing down the treats I had just bought everyone. This fairy tale event ended all too soon, it was time to go back home till next year.

CHAPTER 10

Sometime after I won the fifty cent coin prize money, I won another prize of a different kind. When I was twelve years old, our teacher at school was having unusual spelling bee practice sessions where every day she had two sides competing against each other having us spell a lot of hard words. I was totally ignorant of the fact that she was actually preparing to send one of her students to the upcoming state championship spelling contest, to be held in the nearby town of Linton. I happened to be the student she picked to represent our school, I don't remember being excited, it was all so routine, no fanfare, no compliments, no pat on the back from anybody, so I just did what I was told until I saw mother make me a pretty dress for this occasion, that's when I suspected that something important was about to happen, but I didn't ask any questions. The evening we left for Linton and the spelling bee contest, there was just mom, dad, and myself that were going. I was more excited about having the whole back seat of the car to myself, than I was to wherever we were going. It was a long bumpy ride, going down this gravel highway. When we finally arrived in Linton and entered the auditorium, which was the biggest building I had ever seen in my life, it wasn't long before someone hustled me off away from my parents, into this chaotic atmosphere of what seemed like a thousand kids all in one place. As soon as we were prepared to go on stage, they placed me directly in the front row and I was frantically looking for my parents and was so happy to finally see them sitting in the audience, looking up at me actually having a smile on their faces. I was so relieved that they hadn't forsaken me. Now time to start, a teacher came on stage carrying a thick folder, she would then walk back and forth in front of each row of kids, giving each student their word to spell, if that student spelled that word incorrectly, the teacher would say "down", at which time that student would leave the stage and the teacher would go on to the next student. This was the process of elimination till there were only five of us left on stage, of which I was one. When she came to me with the word "exercise" to spell, I confidently spelled it, "EXSERCISE" and for whatever reason she asked me to spell it again, so I assumed that I had misspelled it, so I quickly changed the "S" to a "C" and spelled it "EXCERCISE", the teacher then said "down", I dashed like a streak of lightning to my parents side. When the contest was over, I was called back on stage and told that I had won fifth place and then was presented with a cross pen and pencil set in a beautiful case, I also received a certificate which I still have today. But the pencil set, mother kept. The trip back home was very quiet, except for the sound of the road gravel banging up against the underside of the car. When we got home everyone had gone to bed so we went to bed as well. My fifteen minutes of fame was over and I slept like a log.

CHAPTER 11

I have great admiration for my parents, for having raised eleven healthy children which I am sure was no easy task under any circumstances, but some of the discipline we received from mother, was far from normal and much of what was unwarranted. She carried out some severe physical beatings on us all at one time or another, which we blindly accepted as normal discipline, unaware of the "WHY" of it all. In hindsight, her problem could have stemmed from the enormous pressure she was regularly subjected to, or she might have carried over her frustrations coming from a home with a very abusive stepfather. These harsh beatings came at random and unexpected for whatever reason. She would always use various objects on us, perhaps a shovel, a big stick, but her favorite was dad's razor strap, which she always kept handy hanging on a nail just inside our pantry door. How I detested that pantry, it always seemed like a bad omen, we never knew what to expect when she headed for the pantry, whether it was time for the razor strap, or some big storm that was coming, or just getting a pot to cook with. This razor strap was made with two heavy leather straps, each four inches wide, held together on one end with a silver metal buckle and this was her favorite end to use on us. One day, she cornered just the two of us, Hildegard and I, in the kitchen, where she first locked the door then she pulled up a chair, grabbed a hold of Hildegard, and laid her across her knees and began to beat her mercifully with this razor strap. I had no way of escaping watching this, knowing that I would be next. As Hildegard kicked and screamed, I went to the coat closet and I picked out the heaviest coat I could find and wrapped it around me. That was a mistake, it made mother so angry, that she not only removed the coat but she removed the rest of my clothes as well. When we went to bed that evening, Hildegard and I were standing in front of the mirror to see if we could find any white skin left on our backs which were totally covered with a mountain of welts and black and blue marks. It was always a traumatic drama to be standing by, having to watch another sibling get beat up and not be able to do anything about it, for fear of repercussions. We still don't know if dad even knew anything about these beatings, because mother would never do it when he was around, or even nearby, and we dared not snitch. Dad's punishment usually didn't amount to much more than him shaking his big fist at us, and we knew he meant business, or maybe he'd give us a slap across the face which usually left an imprint of his huge strong hand. That really was a nice razor strap though, I wish I had it today, "NO" not to keep, but to sell it at the Antique Roadshow!

CHAPTER 12

Being so confined on this farm, we usually invented
our own entertainment, which was mostly done
when our parents had to go to town and we knew
they would be gone for some time. My older
brothers were very good at coming up with all kinds
of antics, sometimes even dangerously so. For
games in the wintertime, the boys would remove
the long handles from our oversized shovels, then
us kids were able to sit down on them and scoot all
over one of the five lakes close by that were frozen
solid. By the time our folks arrived back home, the
shovel handles had all been put back on and the
shovels put in their proper places. Other times, we
would go to the hayloft in the barn, climb up to the
highest rafters and jump down into the hay below
which was stored up there. We would also chase
after and catch sparrows flying around in the loft,
and then we would release them through the open
window and watch them fly happily away.

One day Hildegard and I were outside playing when
we decided to go to one of our tall haystacks to see
which one of us could be the first to climb all the
way to the top, we were racing up the side of this

haystack, laughing and having a great time, when suddenly, a huge bumblebee flew straight into my wide open mouth, then got stuck in my throat and I was not able to cough it up, so I had to swallow it, and I heard it buzzing all the way down my throat. I never climbed another haystack after that. One other day our brother, Ted, told us that he had a surprise show for us and asked us all to gather around this one building. We were all standing there, anxiously looking up at him as he was standing on the roof wearing two large homemade wings strapped to his arms. Then he proudly announced that he could fly like a bird. He opened his arms wide, wings nicely spread apart when he said, "1 -2 – 3 – GO", then, he jumped, but as soon as he cleared the edge of the roof, those fake wings slapped together, over his head, and he splattered flat onto the ground below. Luckily, the only injury he had was a very bruised ego; it was actually a good show that got a lot of laughs. Dad always supplied us with plenty of sleds, but never any skis or ice skates, so we skated on our shoes and the boys made snowboards for us. One winter day, some of us had a contest. We were all on a snowy sloped hill, holding up our sleds to see which one of us could slide out the farthest, on this snow slope with our sleds. When we heard the word "GO" we all plopped down and off we went, laying on our sleds. Art was unfortunate to hit an embedded wire, frozen across his path and his sled stopped dead still, but Art didn't, he finished his run on his belly, and ended up looking like a snowman, no injuries thank God. I don't know where my brothers got their ideas but they always thought of something. This one time they overturned machinery equipment with the wheel exposed on the top, then they tied a long post across the wheel, sat one of us kids on each end of the post, then they'd spin us around as we hung on for dear life, enjoying every minute. Hildegard and I used to build igloos for our playhouse. They were surprisingly warm inside and we were very sad when they began to melt, as soon as the warm weather came along. We would just build new ones the next winter season. I guess we were a tough bunch of kids.

But what we did the most, as soon as our parents left, was make a bee line for our player piano, in our living room. We got a lot of enjoyment out of playing the piano rollers, pedaling away and listening to the beautiful music they made. We all tried to follow the piano keys trying to play the numbers ourselves, and then we'd practice for hours learning to play these numbers. Eventually, we all learned how to play piano without ever having a piano lesson. Some of us became professional musicians playing night club gigs and other celebrations. Mom and dad were both piano players, but they had to control some of our banging on the piano, for we made too much noise. But we made up for it, as soon as they left. Most of us also became accordion players, stemming from the popularity of Lawrence Welk, who actually lived on a farm with his parents, very near our own farm. A lot of locals picked up the accordion also due to Lawrence Welk's popularity. In later years our parents loved to listen to us play.

It was amazing that none of us were ever seriously hurt, or ever got sick very often. The normal childhood diseases that made their rounds, but with all the hard work and roughhousing, there was never a broken leg or a broken arm, never anything more serious than minor cuts & bruises, that were merely treated with liniment and iodine. There was one thing that Dad did to keep his family healthy. He sent for a "Doctor Machine"! This was always our doctor. We never saw a real doctor. This machine was a nice looking cabinet, made of walnut wood, with shelves and drawers. Inside those shelves sat rows of glass jars that were full of a greenish-white fluid solution, I don't know what that was, there were wires protruding out from their sealed lids. The drawers were full of metal attachments, of all sizes & shapes, and they were all covered with a heavy cloth, which had to be wet, when in use, they were then held or tied to the part of your body, that ailed you. After we were successfully hooked up, and the machine was turned on, there was a tingling sensation coming through these attachments, and it was turned up to the degree which you could tolerate. Sometimes, another sibling would sneak up and turn it on full strength, just to hear us scream. We always seemed to leave this machine feeling much better, whether it really did the job, or if it was all of a psychological nature, I don't' know. What I do know is that we never saw a real doctor.

CHAPTER 13

By early fall the crops were ripe and ready for the first phase of harvest. The grain had to be cut down and allowed to dry before the final harvest. This was done by a reaper machine being pulled with dad's little red farm tractor, which mowed down the sheaves, tied them into bundles, and kicked them out onto the mowed fields. Our job was to follow behind the reaper and shock all these bundles of sheaves, which we had to pick up, stand them on their stem ends, with the grain pods on top, for the sun to dry. With the weather always being a factor, it was necessary to work very long days. When we finished the shocked fields looked like there were hundreds of teepees perfectly lined up, which looked so striking that neighbor farmers would compliment dad on what a good job we did. We always did take pride in our work even though it was heavy duty work for us younger ones. Gender didn't seem to matter, boys or girls, did the same kind of work, with little or no help. A funny incident happened one day as Hildegard and I were shocking, when Hildegard picked up one of these bundles and a small water snake, seemingly hiding under it, trying to escape, slithering up under Hildegard's overall pant leg, it slithered all the way up to her chest under her overalls as she tried to grab it, letting out a deafening, curdling scream, which dad heard while driving his tractor nearby. He came running over with this most frightening look on his face, only to see, that by then, Hildegard had already stripped down to her bare panties, she was so embarrassed that she ran to the house for some new clothes. Dad hung his head and slowly walked back to his tractor.

It was sheer torture having to walk on all the fresh cut stubbles left in the fields, and since it wasn't time for new shoes yet, we already had big holes in our soles, our bare feet showing through. So we would cut pieces of cardboard to stuff in there but that only lasted a few steps. We ended up with some very tough bare feet soles.

By the time the bundles were ready for harvest, and with winter already nipping at our heels, it was the custom for some farmers to band together to speed up the process by having more manpower available, the fields were soon buzzing with everyone at their assigned positions, and with all the harvest pollution in the air, the bugs were having a field day, swarms and swarms of big green grasshoppers, hopping around so thick you could hardly open your mouth. They would crawl all over our bodies, underneath our overalls, but we were kept so busy there wasn't a minute we could spare to shoo any of them away.

All the grain bundles we had shocked earlier were now being loaded on to a wagon and taken to a designated location on the farm, where dad operated the threshing machine, which separated the wheat from the chaff. What a joy it was to see dad have this big smile on his face as he watched the whole grains shoot into the wagon, and the nice yellow straw shooting out into huge piles for new mattresses. I was a mere ten years old when dad assigned me a wagon and a team of horses, going back and forth hauling bundles of sheaves, that others had loaded onto my wagon, then another crew would unload it into the threshing machine. It was not an easy task for me to keep control of my team being so close beside this roaring, noisy thresher, while I was being unloaded. If the team gave even a hint of being unruly, dad would shake his big fist at me. Even though I was busy squirming with grasshoppers crawling all over me under my clothes, but I never had a mishap, which I was proud of.

At the end of the day, we would grab handfuls of this new wheat, (grasshopper parts, I suppose) we would then chew on it till it formed into a wad of gluten, it was the only chewing gum we ever got. Besides all the field work, we had to take time to do the chores and get the milking and all the other chores completed, every morning and every evening.

I think our dear mother had the worst job of all. She didn't have to work in the fields, but she spent all of her time in the kitchen, constantly preparing food for the workers. It still puzzles me today, why these workers had to eat so often. The days did start early, we were usually in full swing by sun up, so by 9:00 a.m. mother would have the younger kids bring out a load of food in a little red wagon, which was devoured in minutes. Then at lunchtime, everyone came to the house where mother had prepared another meal for a bunch of hearty eaters. By mid-afternoon mother sent out another red wagon full of food she had prepared. For dinner, mother would have another big meal on the table, after eating we all went back to the fields and worked till it got dark. No doubt, they were very, very long days.

Mother made more noodles in her lifetime than you can stretch from here to New York. Everybody loved them, they were always floating in melted butter and homemade, sautéed croutons, a flavor we haven't been able to match since. When harvest was completed on one farm, we all moved on to the next farmer's farm. Then it became the responsibility of that farmer's wife to cook all those meals for the work crew.

Whatever grains dad didn't sell right away had to be stored in our silo. This silo was just a big round aluminum building that had only one door and a small round window opening near the top, close to the roof. Dad would place a chute into this silo and have wheat come rushing into the silo. While Hildegard and I were placed in the silo, we were given shovels to spread it around evenly as it came pouring in. We were eight and ten year old kids, but we kept up spreading this wheat around as fast as we could, even though the wheat dust was nearly unbearable. The silo became fuller and fuller, the shovel handles were getting shorter and shorter, dad finally had to seal the door and put the chute through the small window near the top, that we were so close to the ceiling we couldn't use our shovels anymore, that's when we had to get down on our hands and knees and move the wheat around using our little bare hands. As the silo was filling up fast, the dust becoming so unbearable that we couldn't breathe anymore, so we made a quick pact that we would take turns crawling to the partially open space that was left open where the chute was coming through; we would fill up our lungs with fresh air, then scoot the wheat around while we were holding our breath till the next turn to get a gulp of air. We were able to hold up that way till we yelled to dad, "the silo is full", by then our backs were hitting the ceiling, I still shudder when I think of how easily we could have suffocated, but we always did look out for each other and kept on going.

With the crops all harvested and winter around the corner, it was time for school to start and finally a new pair of shoes for all of us. Mother would take strips of paper, hold them up to the bottoms of our feet, cut it the length of our foot and put our name on those strips. When it was time to go to town they would match the strips to the new shoes, come home and hand each of us our new pair of shoes. I don't remember any complaints on how they fit, but I do remember a lot of blisters on the back heel of our feet, surely a bad fit. Again no complaints, just happy to have shoes with soles, once again.

CHAPTER 14

One day, for whatever reason, I had an impulse to
find a secluded spot where I could plant one of my
pumpkin seeds that I had saved. I found the perfect
spot and stuck a couple of the pumpkin seeds in the
ground. When I went back a few times, I finally saw
a little green sprout poking through the ground. So
I began to nurture it with love and care, making
sure that no one saw me go there and maybe
discover my secret, for fear they might pull up the
little sprout, just for simple sibling rivalry. It was
growing nicely and one day I saw a little berry on it,
and I knew that this would become a pumpkin. I
was used to watching a lot of things growing on
that farm, but I had a different feeling about this
one, maybe because it was my very own creation,
and I meant to keep it all to myself. I was
surprisingly successful in growing that pumpkin to
maturity, and no one ever discovered my secret.
This pumpkin grew to be so large, I could hardly
carry it. When it was time to figure out what to do
with it as I was so attached to it and didn't want it
destroyed or cut up for some pumpkin pie. So, I
searched and found the perfect place where dad

had stored all of his pumpkins, which was in the grain shed, where they were all lying on top of a heap of stored wheat. When the coast was clear, I carried it to the shed and placed it in on the far end corner away from the rest of the pumpkins. I had proudly mastered my plan and I went to visit my pet pumpkin whenever possible. I would talk to it, pet it, even kiss it sometimes, till I walked in on one of my usual visits and saw that all the pumpkins were gone along with my friend pumpkin. I freaked out, looking for my pumpkin, asking everyone to help me find my pumpkin, they all thought I had gone bonkers, at which time I was forced to confess my secret, and was told that dad had sold all the pumpkins to a man that had come by with a truck. But I knew that Dad had no way of knowing that one of them was my pumpkin, so the damage was done, and I went into mourning.

After the big harvest, dad always saved the corn field for last; bring in the corn. Where we would go into the corn fields, going down each row and retrieve the ears of corn by breaking them off from their stalks, then husk every single one; hundreds, perhaps even thousands, then store to feed to the pigs. All winter long, we would throw some corn over the fence and the pigs would come running for them, gnawing away at the corn, and leaving the empty cobs for us to clean up. Oh how we used to take pleasure in teasing those pigs. One way was where Dad had planted a patch of very tall grass, near the pig pens, for the pigs to roam around in and feed on. So Hildegard and I used to sneak in there, crawl on our hands and knees through the tall grass, where sometimes we'd be crawling flush next to a pig, the grass was so thick they assumed we were just another pig, so at the right moment, we would scream and jump up, just to watch this frightened pig jump two feet high, gyrating in the air. I admit it was a mean trick, but such a good laugh we could use. We also tried to ride them, but their bodies were so round and hard, we usually got bucked off instantly. Then there were the times where Hildegard and I would sit inside their pens, on the side of the open door, waiting for some pig to come wandering in, they couldn't see us till they were nearly all the way in, then we'd clap our hands and once again watch those pigs gyrate into the air, scrambling for a way out. Sorry for the cruel tricks, but the laughs were therapy for us.

CHAPTER 15

Almost in perfect order, year in and year out, there was this continuous trend of doing what comes naturally. Some of this was a nightmare that left me with lifelong scars, yet, with the full understanding of the necessity for sheer survival purposes. As the winters set in, it was slaughter time where they would kill these same animals we had nurtured and played with all year. Being curious youngsters, we would naturally sneak out and watch them slaughter these same animals, the steers, which were once little calves that we fed buckets of milk to, the pig that we used to crawl with, in the tall grass. There is no doubt that it was absolutely sickening, but a way of life that was natural and of which we knew no other. We would watch dad skin these animals before they carried them to the house and plopped on our kitchen table. I can still see this carcass lying on our table with its four stiff legs sticking up in the air. That's where it was then cut up into proper pieces to store as quickly as possible. There was no refrigeration, the only thing we had was a small ice box with a block of ice, sitting under two small shelves. Having no real knowledge of special cuts of steak or roasts, they would just cut the meat into chunks and store it in wooden barrels, covered with a salt water brine so it wouldn't freeze to a solid stage in winter, just slushy enough to be able to pull out a piece when needed. Nothing was ever wasted. Mother cooked the kidneys, the lungs, the liver, and the pig's feet. The skin, the blubber and fat, odds and ends were used to make laundry detergent. Dad would sit and clean intestines for hours to use for sausage, he also cleaned the stomach, which they filled with odd pieces of meats ground up, called head cheese, which actually made good sandwiches if you slathered it with mustard. Dad would smoke whole hams from the hogs, we had a lot of pork roasts, but I never saw any bacon, all the fat was rendered for lard.

Every tidbit that was inedible would be thrown into a big tub to which mother would add a few cans of lye, a little water and boil it. Then she would set it outside and give us kids a big long stick and have us stand there, for hours, stirring this concoction without stopping, till it turned thick and creamy, looking a lot like wet cement. Then she'd let it sit till it set up, at which time she would cut it into bars of soap for laundry day, dish soap and hand soap and for cleaning the kitchen after slaughter was completed. It was a sickening and horrendous experience. It took all of us hours to get it back to normal and get the horrible smell out of that kitchen. I'm convinced that this affected most of the family because they became avid fishermen in later years, and ate a lot of fish.

CHAPTER 16

As the saying goes, "You never miss what you don't have", that is so true, till you finally have it, then you wonder how you ever did without it. We had no electricity of any kind, we always depended on kerosene lanterns or flashlights for all of our lighting, unless it was a full moon, the nights were pitch dark. I still remember the evening when Hildegard and I were making our final trip to the outhouse before bedtime. We were waving around our flashlights and happened to shine them right at, what seemed like, a thousand glass eyes in front of us, all staring back at us. We freaked out and went screaming back to the house, as fast as our wobbly feet would carry us. Dad came looking at all this commotion and discovered a herd of sheep, all perfectly lined up, staring at us. It was later determined that they had all escaped from a nearby sheep herders farm. I don't recall if we needed to go to the outhouse anymore after that.

My brothers were always tinkering at something, either building things or fixing things, they had curious and engineering minds. They came to dad one day and told him that they thought they knew of a way of putting electric lights throughout our house. I guess with dad's okay they successfully accomplished this unbelievable project, as we all watched this whole process with wonder. The first thing they did was built, what we always called a propeller with four blades. This propeller was anchored on the roof of the house, from which they brought a heavy rope through the ceiling in the attic, which we could operate, much like we operated the windmill, which might be where they got the idea, to be able to open and shut it down, depending on the wind, to blow it around and charge the many car batteries that had been placed in the corner of the attic. To watch them string electric wiring through the house was a sight to behold. They wrapped the electric wiring around a cat's body and then they would entice this cat to walk under the already exposed rafters from one end of the house to the other and back, as the wiring unraveled from the cat's body. The end result of this project was an electric cord hanging from the ceiling in every room with an attached light bulb and a chain on the end of it, which we would pull to turn the bulb on or off. When the batteries would run low, the light bulbs would slowly go very dim, that's when someone had to dash to the attic and release the propeller to charge the batteries so the bulbs would brighten right up again. If there happened to be no wind blowing for any length of time, we had to resort back to kerosene lamps, but it was never for very long. This was an unbelievable luxury we really enjoyed, there was no other like it for miles around and news travels fast, we were soon the talk of the town.

CHAPTER 17

During the winter months we had a little more time
to relax, on most evenings. The new lights made
the kitchen cheerfully bright. Mother would come
up with snacks, like her homemade ice cream,
topped with her homemade chocolate sauce and
topped with puffed wheat. Other times we popped
popcorn which we had raised on the farm, which
would pop to large white kernels, with very few
hulls, occasionally mother gave each one of us a big
sunflower bloom and we'd pick out and eat fresh
sunflower seeds, once in a while we each got a glass
of her homemade bread soaked in warm raw milk.
Except for the rich sweet cream and eggs in her
noodles and ice cream, we ate very healthy food,
something they call organic in today's world. We
would run to the garden, pull up carrots and
radishes, wipe the dirt off with our hands, and then
eat them. We'd pick pea pods and eat the delicious
green peas right out of the shell. Dad had a field of
various kinds of melons for us to go and eat all the
melons we wanted. We'd pick one up and crack it
open on our knees, scoop out the seeds and devour
the flesh. If we didn't like one particular melon, we

threw it aside for the bugs to eat, then crack open a different one till we had our fill.

We only got candy and gum when grandma came to visit once a year, but Christmas being the exception. There were no gifts or toys to open, but every Christmas Eve we went to the church Christmas program, where it was mandatory that each child memorize a Christmas verse, which they gave us ahead of time. Then on Christmas Eve we had to stand in the front of the church and orally recite our little poem to the congregation. At the end of the service the men would pass out brown bags filled with goodies for all of the children. In this bag, there was always an orange, the only orange we got all year long. Such a treat, we would only eat one or two sections at a time, so it would last a long time.

After church and retiring on Christmas Eve, we couldn't sleep in anticipation of all the candy we knew we'd receive Christmas morning, where mother would have us all sit in a circle, then she would dole out the goodies of candy and nuts, by dropping them one by one into each of our empty oatmeal boxes which we had saved all year, just for this occasion. The candy and nuts were all loose and everything would stick to the marshmallows and the hard candy. We procrastinated in eating our loot, and mostly playing with it building corrals, using the peanuts, taking the animal crackers, and place them in their proper stalls or pens, so while mother was in the kitchen, baking goodies, cooking meals, the aroma being so intoxicating that put everybody in a good mood. Needless to say, Christmas and the fourth of July were the two days we lived and worked toward all year long.

As the winter was coming to an end, several of the local farmers got together to store ice for summer use. They would go to a local area and dig deep trenches, then they would cut blocks and blocks of ice taken from the frozen lakes, these blocks of ice were then buried in the trenches, layered with straw for insulation. Where everybody had plenty of straw infested ice all summer, for use in our ice boxes, to make ice cream and many other uses. The folks in those days thought of everything, tough, hard working, but seemingly happy people.

Eunice

Marilyn

Annette

My Daughter's High School Pictures

Our farm in North Dakota

The family dog and our North Dakota house

Dad & Mother's first car & first son Ted

Dorothea & Martha at milking time outside of barn

Box sled Dad built – converted to wheels

Leaving for school in box sled now on skis

Shetland pony & cart – Art, Martha, Etta,
Hildegard, Ella & Clifford

Our geese on the North Dakota farm

Art with a new born colt

Art, proud of his snowman

Fall harvest threshing

More threshing grain

Carrying water in the snow

Playing in the snow

Short lived beet thinner invention

My uncle's Model T Ford

Typical Row Crops

Working in the Corn Fields

Day of our auction sale of the North Dakota farm

Art motorized his bike when he was a teenager

Stacking hay

Modern way of stacking hay, it's now baled.

Topping sugar beets

Loading Sacks of Newly Picked Potatoes

CHAPTER 18

Then came that fateful night, a nightmare I wouldn't soon forget. It all started on a very cold winter night, we were all asleep in the attic when we heard our brother Leonard quietly rustling around, waking us up, he motioned for us to be quiet. We had no idea what he was up to, but soon discovered, that he was preparing to run away from home. We were all mortified, in the middle of winter, snowing, very cold, where was he going to go, out into nowhere? He didn't answer any questions, just kept putting on layers and layers of clothes, there was no suitcase for him to pack, he finally put on what we called a "sheep coat", the warmest coat in existence at the time. Then he quietly started going down the stairs, we all followed behind, and were shocked to see mom and dad already up, sitting in the kitchen, reading the Bible, tears running down their faces. They must have gotten wind of it beforehand. They had locked the door and wouldn't let Leonard leave, hanging on to him, crying, pleading with him, not to do this. A most distressful scene to say the least, as we all stood silently and helplessly watching this whole scenario. The very last thing we saw was Leonard raising up the window and starting to crawl out, mom and dad trying to pull him back in as they were sobbing loudly. Leonard succeeded and slipped on through the window, into the pitch dark cold night and disappeared. We all went back to bed, crying and spent a sleepless night. As I'll talk about later in the book, I'm convinced that it was actually a blessing in disguise. After that, Mom and dad were very gloomy and things weren't the same as we all went about our business.

It wasn't till many years later when Leonard told us what happened that night. He said that he and his buddy had this all planned out ahead of time. After he climbed out the window, he had someone waiting to take them to the little town of Hague, where they hopped, undetected, to the top of a freight train heading for Montana. He said as the train began to move faster and faster, the ice cold wind was fiercely hitting then in the face and they were beginning to fear that they might freeze to death before they could reach Montana. They began to pray, when all of a sudden, a huge piece of cardboard came flying right towards them, they both grabbed for it and were able to catch it, which they then used to shield themselves with from the cold wind, and they think it probably saved their lives. The guardian angels made sure of that. He said, they made it to Montana and soon found jobs. At home, Leonard had left a big void and we missed him terribly. Mom and dad looked very gloomy and worried. There was no spunk left in any of us, but we needed to go on, even doing Leonard's share of the work. We were unaware of any kind of communication going on between Leonard and our parents, but we were very happy to see him when he finally came home for a visit and we all hoped he'd stay this time, "Not to be", instead, our other brother Ted, went back with him, this time very amicably, with the blessing of mom and dad, but they had no choice, it was out of their control. This time the boys headed for California to start a new life there, which had been Leonard's original idea. We knew they were communicating with mom and dad after that, but we had no knowledge of what was transpiring. We were told that they made it as far as Idaho, loved it there, and decided to stay there where they started a trucking business, hauling hay for the local farmers. One summer, mom and dad made a trip to Idaho to visit the boys. They also liked Idaho, a lot, they were very impressed with the many fruit trees they saw and the nice weather, they came home looking relaxed and happy, but shared little else about their trip, except what we overheard in their conversations and the now unusual smiles on their faces. Not much later, everything became a hustle and a bustle throughout the farm,"very unusual", dad was busy cleaning out sheds, having us help toss things here and there, when I heard him say "oh yes, that goes too, I'm selling everything at this auction sale"!!! I froze in my tracks, did I hear right, "Selling everything, does that include us"? As he looked at me and said "close those big eyes of yours before your eyeballs fall to the ground and get back to work"!! Little by little things became real, we soon learned that the farm had already been sold and we were all moving to Idaho! I was totally oblivious of what lie ahead; Idaho could have been across the street for all I knew. We muddled like robots through this whole crazy transition, as it slowly evolved. The morning of the auction sale, more cars and trucks began to pull into the yard than I ever thought existed. People began to snoop around looking at our stuff and then things were really going crazy when I saw this nicely dressed man standing behind a podium, waving his hands and shouting at the top of his voice, which sounded like he had a speech problem. Art was having some fun watching people getting tangled in our sagging clotheslines. He decided to have more fun, when he took dad's car batteries, which dad had used to slightly electrify some of our barbed wire fences, just to deter livestock from straying, Art hooked them to the clothesline, then we sat back and giggled as we watched people touch these clotheslines and flinch. Also, this fellow was selling popcorn, having his supplies in his car, so Art electrified his car that became such a nuisance for the popcorn man every time he touched it, he got a jolt. He offered us free popcorn if Art would unhook it.

Pretty soon things weren't so funny anymore. People were hauling away truckloads of our livestock, watching the horses, cows, and pigs looking back at us, pigs squealing, a very emotional scene. I guess dad was lucky to have sold everything by the end of the day because the place looked forsaken, like a ghost town. Debris was blowing around, empty popcorn boxes, papers, twigs and weeds. All that was left were the clothes on our backs. Leonard had come home, bringing one of his trucks to help us move. It had already been loaded ahead of time, ready to head out. Dad couldn't part with is little red Farmall tractor, so that was put on the truck first, the next thing they loaded was our big player piano, no room left except for a few boxes, odds and ends, that small truck was so overloaded you could actually see it sag in the middle.

The sale now over, everyone had taken their goods and left. Dad rounded us up, ready to go, it was a sad moment to walk away from the only home and security I'd ever known. We all said our goodbyes at the outhouse. Leonard took our brother, Art, with him in the truck and with the exception of our sister, Esther; who had a commitment for another year to teach school before she joined us a year later, we all piled into dad's 1938 Ford two-door sedan, mom and dad were in the front seat, Betty on mother's lap, Dorthea, Martha, Myself, Hildegard, Ella, and Clifford, a guitar and mother's pet cat in a crate and of course our guardian angel, were all in the back seat. The guitar was lying across the back space by the rear window. The cat, in her crate, was directly on the floor in front of me where my knees were now in my face. Just before my father got in the car, I saw him place a little red metal box under the driver's seat. I learned much later that it contained the entire cash he had taken in from the auction sale that day. I'm guessing, possibly, his entire worth at the moment. I can't imagine what must have gone through his mind as he was driving away from that farm. I'll never forget my own mixed emotions as I turned around to take a final look out the rear window and what I saw, was one last car sitting there, it's door hanging open and the new owner of our dog, Rexy, was pulling on his leash with all his might, trying to get this struggling dog to get into the car, while Rexy was hanging back with all of his strength, whining loudly, not cooperating at all, just as dad drove over the hill and out of sight. This haunted me for some years. The people that had purchased our farm had given us an open invitation to come visit anytime anyone of us wanted to. Through the years my parents and some siblings had gone back to visit several times, but I never had the desire to go back till some fifty years later. (More about that visit later in the book.)

We were well on our way now, bumping along the gravel road, going to my aunt's house, who would put us up for the night; very noble of her to take in such a clan. As it all turned out, Leonard wasn't running away from home that fateful night, he went looking for greener pastures for the family. The next morning we all piled back in the car and following Leonard in his truck, we headed for this place called Idaho, which really should have been a happy adventure, but I didn't see one bit of excitement around me. Everyone seemed to be soberly quiet. I was seated on the extreme left side, in the back seat, directly behind the driver.

Some time into this trip, it was pouring down rain, dad was approaching a curve in the road, when the oncoming car couldn't completely make the curve, and clipped our car, on the left rear, exactly where I was sitting, our car went spinning all over the place, but dad soon had it under control and we ended up in a ditch. With Leonard in the truck in front of us, he stopped, they looked at the damage, the tire was all in shreds, and it was a miracle no one was injured. That blessed guardian angel saw to that again. I don't remember all the details, getting it fixed, but it kept raining very heavily. We were finally on our way again, but not for too long. As we approached the small town of Mandan, the axle broke on Leonard's overloaded truck, no surprise there! We had traveled less than a hundred miles by then and I suppose dad figured we were in for a long wait getting that truck fixed, so he parked his family near the city park in Mandan. What a relief, to be able to climb out of the crowded car, to run in the park and roll on all this plush green grass, no dirt to speak of, sidewalks to walk on, swings and see saws to play on, tables where mother could lay out her ever present bologna sandwiches for lunch.

It was glorious. It took most of the day to get the truck repaired but we did leave and travel a bit more, but not too long before dad stopped for us to spend the night in a hotel. In the chaos of getting everybody settled in, somehow mother's pet cat got out of her cage and disappeared into the night. We all searched and searched for her, using our flashlights, but we were unable to find her. Mother was very sad, but we had no other choice but to leave the cat behind. The one positive thing that came out of that, was, I was now able to sit with my feet on the floor.

CHAPTER 19

I don't remember how much longer we traveled, but the rest of the trip was uneventful, other than being crammed like sardines, without a peep of a complaint. We had a lot of time to think and I wondered where all this was going to take us. So far we were still in the dark, nothing had been explained to us. In the month of July, 1941, we arrived in the small town of Paul, Idaho, where my brothers were staying at the time. Dad hadn't wasted any time in purchasing another farm, which was located in Declo, a few miles away. Since it wouldn't be ready to occupy for some time, Dad rented a home for us in the city of Rupert. The culture shock of everything around us, neighbors so close, people everywhere, took a lot of getting used to or even to believe, like turning on a faucet and have water come running out was a miracle. No windmill, no buckets, where did this water come from? How come some of it was already hot? It was unbelievable to be told that we could always have it that way now. The bathroom with this nice white tub, always ready with hot water, to take a bath as often as you like. The all white toilet, how could this work with just a touch of a little handle, we still have to laugh about what our father said the day he saw our neighbors have a cookout on their patio, he said, "What's the world coming to, we used to shit outside and eat in the house, now we're shitting inside the house and eating outside!" It sounded like he was trying to adapt as much as we were. Mother was so happy with the cupboards everywhere and the counter space everywhere. She was already more relaxed and hadn't beaten us for a while now. It was near time for school to start, and there were three of us going to school at the time, myself, Hildegard, and Ella. Clifford and Betty were still too young. Being the oldest, I was still responsible for the younger ones. I was starting eighth grade; Hildegard was in seventh grade and Ella in second grade. The school happened to be conveniently located only one block from our house we were renting, (it is necessary for me to backtrack a bit at this point.)

I need to clarify a matter about the confusion of my name, all the previous years. Since I had been born at home with no doctor present, I didn't have a birth certificate, although I did have a baptismal certificate. The day I was baptized and the preacher asked my mother what she wished to name me, she said "A-dah", the German sound of my name, and consequently my name was entered on my baptism certificate as "Eda". So I always answered to "A-dah" till I started school. I still don't know why this happened or why it was allowed to go on, all the years I attended school in North Dakota, but every year I went to school there, they couldn't seem to get my name right. Every school year I had this burden with my name. Maybe it was the language barrier, at the time, but every school year I had a different name. One year I was Eda, another year I was called Edith, another I was Etha, then Edna, and on it went. I just got accustomed to answer to whatever I was called that year, but I was always wondering, and I never asked, why I had so many different names, when my siblings only had one.

This brings me back to that very first day of school, in our new surroundings in Rupert, Idaho. Mother must have been as frustrated about my name as I had been because the first day of school, just before she shoved us out the door to walk to school, she pulled me aside, she took my hand in hers, then pressed this little crumbled piece of white paper into the palm of my hand, she closed my fist tightly, then sternly looked me in the eye and with a twinge of anger in her voice she said to me, "des ish dy naama!" (Translation) "This is your name!" As I walked away, I was thinking, "What!" Another name, I have so many already. I could hardly wait to get some distance from the house, when I took the piece of paper, unfolded it gently, and saw in bold print my new and permanent name, "ETTA"! I liked it a lot and held on to that scrap of paper for dear life, so I wouldn't lose it and have to start all over again. I'm thinking mother had been as frustrated as I was all those years and finally decided to correct it. As we walked the short distance to school, the sun shining bright, sidewalks, fresh cut green grass, no dirt clods to stumble over, no barbed wire fences to have to climb under, and best of all, "no bull to run from"! It was exhilarating to say the least. As we reached the school grounds, I saw a million kids running wild and crazy as I was still wondering where the one room school was among all this chaos. Then I saw the stairs, that looked like they were going to heaven, but we all held hands and started to climb up and go through two of the biggest doors I'd ever seen in my life. Once inside, I looked up and down the longest hall that reminded me of a wheat field, and doors everywhere. I thought, through one of those doors has to be our one room school house.

Just then the school bell rang so loud that we froze in our tracks, watching all these crazy kids being swallowed up through all those doors in minutes. I wondered if we should've been running with them or not. Just as quick, it became eerily quiet, so I walked my sisters to this furnace against a wall in the hallway, and we just stood there hanging on to each other. I had no clue of where to go from there when I finally saw this neatly dressed man in a suit and tie, come walking towards us. I had never heard of a principal's office, as a matter of fact, I had never heard of a principal before. He stopped and looked at us, and by then, I would think, we probably looked like three scared lambs, standing in the dark, looking into the headlights of an oncoming car. But he was so very nice and took us to his office. As he began asking us all these questions, it soon became obvious that nothing had been done in the way of a transfer from our North Dakota school. I was so in the dark, that I was no help at all, other than to tell him what grade each of us were to be in. When he got to the part where he asked me my name, I happily said, "I'm glad you asked because I just found out myself"! I then pulled out the little piece of white crumbled paper I had in my pocket, I neatly unfolded it then held it up for him to read. About that time he started to speed up the paperwork, leering at me out of the corner of his eye. Maybe he wondered if we were from Mars, and I don't suspect he was far off. He finally placed us in our proper rooms and I was shocked that every person in my room was also in the eighth grade. But it wasn't too long before we were running with the rest of the crazies down the hall. No one at home ever asked us how our first day at school had gone; maybe mother figured it out when she saw my underpants on laundry day.

After a couple of months of living in Rupert, we moved to our new farm in Declo. This time I went to the principal and told him we were moving and he made a smooth transition for us to the Declo school. I guess that was lesson number one for me. I didn't want to be thrown into the den of lions a second time. I was much more prepared, but what I wasn't prepared for was that we now had to ride a bus to school. I nosed around from the neighbor kids about the bus schedule so the three of us were at the proper bus stop that first morning, along with a few other kids. I was very nervous when this big yellow car pulled up. The doors flew open, but I held on to Hildegard and Ella till the other kids got on first and when I finally stepped in and saw all those seats, my first thought was, "we sure could've used this car on our trip here from North Dakota"! The school was located in downtown Declo, on the far end of Main Street where all the merchants were. It was convenient for the students to run to town at lunchtime to buy goodies or lunch. I soon learned to run with them, I was learning a lot, I'm just glad they never ran to the edge of a cliff. Since we never got to go to town except that once a year in Hague, North Dakota for the fourth of July celebration, and even then we never saw the inside of a store, except the ice cream shop. So we had a field day going from store to store, we never had any money to buy anything with, but we had a field day looking around. Hildegard and I still laugh about the day we were nosing around, at lunchtime, when we walked into a beauty shop there. We were looking at all the movie star pictures hanging on the wall with the most exotic hairdos we'd ever seen. We asked the fellow there if he could really do all those hair styles and he said that he could. We were so enamored that we told mother about it when we got home and asked her if we could have our hair done like that. She gave each of us a quarter and said go ahead. The next day, Hildegard and I took off for the beauty shop at lunchtime, we looked and looked at all these beautiful hairdos and finally picked the ones we wanted. So the fellow worked on both of us, giving us the style we picked. He first cut our beautiful long hair then plastered our hair flush against our scalp with globs of gel and made huge waves flat against our heads. We thought we were so pretty as we ran back to school and ended up being late, lunchtime was long over, we proudly walked into our rooms late and wondered why everybody kept staring at us. We must have been some sight, out beautiful long hair all cut off and our short hair plastered against our scalps with tons of gel. I think we thought the stares were because we looked like one of them movie stars hanging on the wall at the beauty shop. I don't remember what mother's reaction was when we got home but I think she turned her head, so we couldn't see that she was laughing. At the Rupert school we were so close to home, we always ran home for lunch, but in Declo mother packed us lunches. With my eyes wide open, I noticed a lot of kids buying lunch at the cafeteria, which I'd never seen before; I told mother we could buy lunches at school. So the next morning she gave me a dime to buy all three of our lunches with. I had no idea the cost of this cafeteria, so off I went with the dime for our lunch that day, for all three of us. The minute the bell rang, we ran with the crowd to the cafeteria, I was looking forward to this new experience. When I got up to pay, the girl said "that will be fifteen cents", five cents each. I only had a dime and she said, "Too bad." I took Hildegard and Ella by the hand and we ran to town with some of the other crazies, we walked into the grocery store there and we looked and looked to see what we could buy for ten cents that would feed all three of us. The only thing I found that would fit the bill was a small loaf of Weber's bread. So I purchased it and we left to go back to the school to eat it. The minute we stepped out the front door of this grocery store, their huge store sign above the entrance came crashing down, having been blown down from the strong winds. It barely missed my head, but grazed my shoulder, as it crashed onto the sidewalk. About that time, the store manager came running out of the store, his eyes wide open and asked me if I was alright. With everything else I'd been dealing with I said, "I'm fine, why do you ask? Isn't this normal?" My new name "Etta" did make the newspaper the next day. We proceeded to walk back to school and again stood by the heater against the wall in the hallway.

Too embarrassed to show this loaf of bread, that was our lunch, I kept it under my coat and doled it out slice by slice as we stood there and devoured the whole loaf. Actually, it was a real treat for us because at home we never got anything but homemade bread.

We were now happily settled in our new Declo farm, we loved the milder Idaho winters, dad was very content as he bustled around getting his farm ready for Spring planting and learning this whole new way of farming from what we were used to.

Mother looked happy and relaxed, having more modern facilities now, and was even able to grab a nap now and then, which I never saw her do in North Dakota. It was a new and wonderful life, but it didn't last very long. The whole atmosphere took a complete turn one Sunday morning on December 7, 1941, the Pearl Harbor attack, which seemed to change the mood all around. There were four sons in our family and Ted was soon drafted into the army, Leonard had a kidney disease and didn't have to go to war, Art joined the navy, Esther, the oldest sister, got married, so the family was shrinking at a rapid pace that took its toll on our parents. I was still young and naïve and didn't understand most of what was happening, so I asked mother one day what all this talk was about a war. The way she explained it to me was to say, "A bunch of soldiers are running around and killing people with rifles and bayonets. I took that very serious and started having nightmares about soldiers chasing me with their bayonets, till I learned more facts at school about what it was really all about. I was unprepared when a group of kids cornered me at school one day, taunting me, poking me, asking where I was born, I told them North Dakota, they wanted to know why I had an accent, I didn't even know what they were talking about. I hadn't even known my own name all those years, I surely didn't know what they meant by an accent. They wanted to know why I didn't salute the flag. That was news to me, I saluted the flag every morning with the rest of the students, and I told them to watch me. They finally just walked away, looking back at me; I was at a total loss as to what this was all about. I know now, I was pretty lucky. Like they say, "ignorance is bliss". I never told anyone about this, but I made it a point to keep my distance from those kids after that.

Life at home was somber, mother was crying a lot, but dad kept us busy getting the farm ready for spring planting. Working this new Idaho farm was a complete turnaround from what we were used to. Instead of picking rocks and burning tumbleweeds, we needed to stand in a cold potato cellar and cut up truckloads of potatoes for planting seed. We had to stand along this long narrow table, which had embedded razor sharp knives along one side, the sharp edges facing away from you, as we were wearing heavy gloves, we would pick up a potato from the pile in front of us and slam it into this sharp knife which would cut this potato into small pieces, and we had to make sure each piece was left with at least one potato eye. It was surprising how good we got at this after a few truckloads of potatoes. We got cold and tired from standing in those cellars for hours at a time, but the work was always done, or else!

On this new Idaho farm in Declo, all of us had to learn a whole new way of farming from what we were used to on our North Dakota farm, where after spring planting we just waited for the rains to take care of the watering, but on our new Declo farm, we planted row crops of sugar beets, potatoes, and beans, and they needed irrigation on a regular basis till harvest time. What I hated worse than that was having to thin the sugar beets as soon as they started to sprout and grow. They came up very thick and it was vital that they needed to be thinned out, which we called "beet thinning". We had to crawl on our hands and knees, using a short handled hoe and hoe out all the beets and leave only one plant about every 15 inches or so. This gave that one beet plant room to grow into a huge sugar beet, making for a good crop. If you left more than one plant, it would grow and snarl around each other. Not good. This was slow and tedious work from sun up to sun down. We hardly ever looked up to see the acres and acres of beets still ahead of us to be thinned. There was no dilly-dallying allowed, they were growing fast and time was of the essence. My brothers decided that there had to be an easier way of doing this, so they actually built a one of a kind beet thinning machine. It was motorized and it seated four people as it slowly crawled us up and down the field as we thinned beets, sitting down. Unfortunately, they thought of it too late because eventually they came out with a way to plant these sugar beets already spaced fifteen inches apart, so the invention became obsolete before it got off the ground. Work was never ending, as soon as the thinning was completed, we had to return to these same fields, with long handled hoes now, and hoe out all the weeds that were trying to take over. This had to be done as long as the weeds kept growing. Also, these crops needed to be watered on a regular basis.

The water came from the Snake River that filled up the canals that were everywhere, and that water was rationed to each farmer, at particular times through the season, and you had better take advantage of it or lose your turn till the next time, which was a no no. When we had our turn, we'd go out wearing our hip boots and carrying big shovels, as soon as the water came running through the ditches throughout the farm, we had to guide and control this water so it would run down every single row of crops. This meant shoveling mud to close up each row after the water filled it up, and open up another row. Many times you worked all night. It did make me think, that this was a step up from shoveling manure in North Dakota. It makes me feel good to see the farmers having huge sprinkler systems spraying water on their crops today! Where were they when we needed them!

CHAPTER 20

At our Declo farm, we had a lot less livestock than we had in North Dakota. There was the necessary team of horses, three or four cows for our dairy needs, several pigs (dad's favorite), always dogs and cats, and chickens that were underfoot all the time, we had an abundance of eggs for mother to use, as she was still making noodles and the delicious chicken noodle soup, every Sunday without fail. Most of us girls still make chicken noodle soup on Sunday, but that's a good habit. In Idaho, other than killing a chicken once in a while, there were no more slaughter days to deal with, dad would just take the steer to the slaughter house and come home with the meat all packaged up for the freezer. Dad also raised alfalfa (hay), and that needed to be harvested two or three times a season, which had to be worked in with everything else we had to do. Dad would go out with his little red tractor and mow down the nice green alfalfa, after which we raked it into huge heaps, then left if for a few days to dry out, then came the hard part again as we went out with our pitchforks to pick up these heaps of hay and pitch them up onto a wagon, where dad always placed Hildegard to stack it evenly around so it wouldn't shift. Hildegard had a reputation of being the best hay stacker around. Her wagons were always stacked perfectly straight and when we unloaded, her finished hay stacks always looked like a perfect loaf of bread; we never had a hay stack that leaned or was crooked, like you could see on some other farms, where some needed to be braced to keep from falling over. We still have to laugh about the time Hildegard, dad and I were unloading this load of hay from the wagon, I was in control of the big crane with this huge fork dangling at one end, which I was operating from the little red tractor, I would let it down to the wagon then dad would grab it and clamp it into a clump of hay, and secure it. When he gave me the OK signal and I'd pull it up, swing it over and dump it on the hay stack where Hildegard would spread it around, then I'd bring the fork back to dad where he would repeat the process. This one time I saw him clamp it down and for some reason I must've missed his proper signal, and I started to pull it up, up, up, when all of a sudden I saw dad's legs sticking out, hanging from the fork, frantically kicking away in mid air. I immediately swung him back and let him down on the wagon, and then I waited for my punishment, but surprisingly, it never came. He never said a word and we went about our business. I still think he had to be laughing, which we couldn't see. Hildegard and I sure had a big laugh, talking about it afterwards.

CHAPTER 21

Fall was approaching and it was time to harvest the sugar beet crop and potato fields we had nurtured all summer and watched them grow into a good crop. Dad would first go into the beet fields with his little red tractor and loosen up the beets that had grown very large and deep into the ground, so to make it easier for us to pull them out and top them off, we always worked with a partner alongside you, where we each straddled three rows of beets, carrying a long machete sharp knife, which had a large sharp hook on the end of it, which we used to hack into the beet and yank it out of the ground the rest of the way, then we'd sling it over one knee, and whack off the big green top with the sharp knife. This definitely required a certain amount of precision, if you wanted your legs left in one piece by the end of the day. After the beets were topped, we threw them into the rows between us, ready for loading when the truck came by, when we had to stop topping long enough to load the truck which dad then took to the local sugar factory. They all had to be loaded all by hand as the truck rolled slowly along, with a crew on each side, we'd stoop down, pick up the beet and hurl them up on to the truck, stoop and hurl, stoop and hurl, till the truck was full to the brim, sometimes so full that some of those large beets would roll back down and hit us on the back of the head while we were stooped over to pick up another beet, it downright stunned us. But luckily, there were never any casualties with any serious head injuries, we think!!!

As soon as we finished fields and fields of beet topping, we were moved to the potato fields, many times on the same day. There wasn't time for rest periods, the crops needed to be out before any frost season might sneak up on us. Dad, again on his little red tractor with some equipment, we called the "little potato digger", with which he'd go up and down the rows of potatoes and the little digger would scoop them up out of the ground where the potatoes were now exposed on the surface, waiting to be hand picked. Again, we worked with a partner where we each took a row of potatoes and large wire baskets pinched between our legs, we stooped over and picked up each and every potato lying on the ground, filling up the baskets, then stop and empty their contents into a burlap sack that had already been strewn, at intervals, for our convenience. We picked steadily all day, except when the truck came by periodically, then we had to load up the sacks of potatoes to be taken to the potato cellars. Again, there was a crew on each side of the truck bed and we'd have to pick up the sacks of potatoes and hurl them on to the truck bed. Those sacks weighed anywhere from fifty to seventy pounds, which made it back breaking work for us young teenage girls. Nevertheless, we had to keep up till the work was done. We always tried to get a partner that picked about the same pace you yourself did, or it could become very frustrating, especially if we picked for other farmers and got paid for it. The faster we picked the more money we made.

Dad would never hire any outside help; he had raised a good work crew himself. But he had no problem hiring us out to other farmers that needed potato pickers; because we always finished our fields first. Being hired out we were paid fifteen cents a basket so Hildegard and I stayed partners, cause we were both fast and we couldn't tolerate slow pickers, they held you back too much. For some reason, dad was kind enough to let us keep some of the money we were being paid. So one season, Hildegard and I had saved $75.00 between us. We felt so rich but didn't know what to do with it. It would've been a waste to squander it so we picked up the Sears Roebuck catalog that was always lying around the house. It was so full of choices, all those beautiful clothes, no! We thought those weren't necessary, then we saw pages and pages of jewelry, oh no, we said, those are for movie stars, besides which, it wouldn't look good with bib overalls, but we agreed that it would surely glisten under the sun in those fields. Then we saw shoes of all kinds, no! folks bought those for us, finally we came to pages and pages of typewriters. That perked up our eyes and ears because we were both taking typing in school at the time, so we ordered a Remington typewriter which cost $69.95 + tax. That pretty much ate up our $75.00, but we thought it was worth every potato we picked, we really loved it and we shared ownership of that typewriter for years, my house, then her house, her house, then my house. Neither of us remembers what ever happened to it in the end. It would be worthless in today's world anyways.

CHAPTER 22

I would like to explain my reasoning for bringing up the little red tractor so often. It seemed to be such a part of the family, following us all the way from North Dakota to Idaho; it almost seemed like another sibling. Working right alongside of us all those years without fail, and it didn't retire until we retired. It must have been the best tractor that Farmall ever built. Although at the last, it was beginning to remind me of the little choo choo train, "I think I can, I think I can"! Long after I left home and moved away, and had come home on one of my visits, I happened to see it parked behind the barn. I got on it and was surprised that it started up, so I backed out and took a short spin around the yard; I'd forgotten what a rough ride it was, I almost lost my insides as I bounced around on it. It is still parked today on my nephew's farm. It doesn't look so red anymore, faded from sitting in the full sun. That's where it will probably stay till whenever, but it's still nice to get to look at it at times; I have four brothers and two sisters that stayed in the farming business and did very well.

CHAPTER 23

I liked going to school and I was getting very good grades, I still have my diplomas that I've saved all these years. In May 1942, I graduated from eighth grade at Declo. I was very excited when mother sewed me a beautiful blue and white brocade A-line type dress for the occasion. I also curled my shoulder length shiny red hair, into a page boy style, using a curling iron that needed to be heated in the hot coals on the kitchen stove. I thought it looked becoming on me, as I looked in the mirror and thought that I actually looked quite pretty. I'd never felt so feminine before and felt like maybe I was growing up. I was extremely happy to see my parents actually get dressed up and come to my graduation. I felt like it was their way of telling us how proud they really were of us, because they never verbally praised us for anything we did, but I think it was always in their hearts, and as they say, "you never miss what you don't have"! And we didn't but later in life it all came together. They truly had been very proud of their children all along. I think that worked both ways. I'm not sure that any of us ever told them we loved them, as we were growing up, but we all made up for it being a very, very close family for many years and it has been very hard on us to see some of them leave this world, but I'm sure we'll all be a happy clan, in heaven some day.

CHAPTER 24

The fall of 1942, I started my freshman year at Declo High School, which happened to be conveniently located right next door to the elementary school I had just completed. Hildegard was in eighth grade, Ella was in fourth grade, and my little brother, Clifford, was beginning first grade that year. I was so happy being in high school, I had nice friends, good teachers, I thought life couldn't be any better, UNTIL... I came home from school one day and was told that dad had sold the farm and we would be moving back to Rupert, where dad had already purchased a smaller forty acre farm, about four miles out of Rupert, but at the same time, he also purchased a twelve acre parcel on the outskirts of Rupert which had a large two story house, a barn, and a chicken coop; that's where we would live. So in 1943, after two years in Declo, we moved back to Rupert. I suppose the family was dwindling at such a rapid pace and dad was losing most of his work crew, so he downsized to a smaller farm. But when I did my math, it seemed to me that six people working an eighty acre farm, and three people working a forty acre farm came out to about the same amount of work for each. With the older boys gone to war, Esther and Dorothea now married, Martha getting married, that left me at the age of fifteen, the oldest of five children still living at home. Dad still wouldn't hire any outside help, so that left dad, myself and Hildegard to work the farm. Ella, Clifford, and Betty soon got their share of very hard work on this new forty acre farm. No matter how young, if we could walk, we worked. Dad always told his children that he bought the twelve acres in town as insurance for his children, in case of a famine; we would be able to be sustained, raising our own food. Sadly, the property eventually sold, but the way things look today, I wonder if he knew something we didn't. I still have a lot of relatives in the farming business that would come to our rescue, so I hope he rests well.

Our place in Rupert, where we lived, happened to be located right next door to a florist business called "Henshields Florist and Greenhouse". They grew a lot of their own flowers and vegetable starter plants to sell. Sometimes they would hire us kids to help plant all those little starter plants in little pots, they were very happy to have us because there was no training required, we knew how to work in the dirt and we were fast. Now it was time for school to start, this would be the third time we changed schools in two years time. The high school in Rupert and the elementary school were again conveniently located across the street from each other and were very close to downtown Rupert, which we called the town square. I was now a sophomore, Hildegard a freshman, Ella was in fourth grade and Clifford was in second grade. Betty was still too young to go to school. Since I was the oldest sibling at home now, it became my responsibility to get up early every morning, when dad got up, and have breakfast ready when he came in from milking the few cows we still had for our dairy needs. This allowed mother to be able to sleep in. Then came the first day we were to start going to our new schools. I had everybody ready, our lunches were packed and we were on time at the designated bus stop. When the bus pulled up, we all piled in and were off to a new adventure and actually it did turn out to be a little bit of an adventure for me before it was all over. When we arrived at school, Hildegard went across the street to the high school to start her freshman year, but again I had the responsibility to take Ella and Clifford across the street to the elementary school to place them in their proper rooms, again with the help of the principal. This was a big change for them and they needed more of my moral support than I'd expected, so I stayed with them longer, till I felt comfortable about leaving them, by then it was too late for me to go across the street and start my day at the new high school, so I decided to wait and start the next morning and just walk home for now, but as I looked around, I had no clue of where I was or even which way to start walking. Everything was strange to me, I had no clue what my new address was, we had no telephone, so I began to panic, I thought I was lost. I decided to go back into the school and told the principal about my dilemma. He was very kind, he asked me some questions about where I live and I couldn't answer any of them. He walked me outside and pointed this way and that way, and I stood there like a dumbbell, having not a clue. He scratched his head and was beginning to look as worried as I was, then all of a sudden; I remembered to tell him that we lived next door to "Henshields Florist and Greenhouse". Then his face lit up like he had just hit the lottery and with a smile on his face, he took me to his office and drew me a map to follow then I walked home. I took off walking and praying, following the map, and made it home safely. I often wondered if that principal ever waited for news about a little girl being lost out there somewhere. Needless to say, I have a lot of respect for principals, they were always there when I needed them and boy did I need them!

CHAPTER 25

Spring was coming and it was time to go to work on our new Rupert farm for spring planting. I wished we didn't have to farm anymore, but dad had five more children to raise and farming was all he knew, even though he was getting up in years by now and mother was beginning to have health problems. This time it was a hassle because we had to make the commute to the farm everyday. Dad would take Hildegard and drive out in the car and leave me to harness and hitch the team of horses to the wagon, and bring supplies for the day. So every morning I went trotting down the main highway, cars whizzing by, some were honking and waving, but I don't remember seeing any fingers. It wasn't unusual to see tractors pulling equipment down the highway, but very few horses and wagons. Our first job in the spring was to clean out all the ditches that were running throughout the farm, for irrigation purposes. They would be so overgrown with weeds from the winter snow, that you could hardly see the ditch. There would be all these little water snakes come scurrying out as we dug away with our shovels and they'd scare us to death. Dad would be on his little red tractor, plowing the fields and one of us would have to stop digging ditches and hitch the horses to the harrow, that had long sharp teeth, which we had to walk behind as it was being pulled back and forth these newly plowed fields to break up the clods and make it a smooth field for planting. We probably walked multiple miles a day that way, we didn't need any treadmills. I was very surprised one day when I got home from school, dad took me to the barn to show me a new team of horses he had bought that day and had sold our regular team we had. I couldn't believe what I saw, when I looked at two of the biggest horses I'd ever seen. They reminded me of those big Clydesdales; their hooves looked as big around as our dining room table. I almost got sick to my stomach, but I refrained from saying anything, yet!! They looked like I'd need a ladder to harness them, saying nothing yet not being used to speaking up for ourselves; I just went back to the house. It bothered me and I actually had a sleepless night and wondered how I was going to get out of this one. For some reason, the next morning, I finally blurted out to dad and said, "Those horses out there frighten me to death and I will not harness them nor bring them out to the farm this morning or any other morning, for that matter"! I was ready for whatever punishment he saw fit, but he rather surprised me when he sharply turned around and headed for the barn, of course, I just followed him. I watched as he harnessed up those horses, hitched them to the wagon, then he jumped onto the wagon, looked at me and sternly said, "Well then you bring the car out"! He was well aware of the fact that I had never driven an automobile before. I was a little stunned, but I soon decided that if he thought he was threatening me, he was dead wrong. I walked to the car, which was a stick shift, I had no driver's license, I told Hildegard to get in the passenger seat, I got in the driver's seat and off we went weaving down the road, coming within inches of hitting a tree as we left the yard, and I yelled, "Hildegard, watch out!" She yelled back, "You're the one that's driving!" I made it to the farm safe and sound and that's the way it was done every morning, UNTIL... not that long afterwards, dad left the yard with those big horses and came back with two mules. Maybe he thought I'll give this stubborn one two more stubborns. I actually came to the conclusion that he wasn't all that happy with those big horses himself. The two mules then became my lot till the end of my farming days. I really didn't mind them at all, except it was the only time that I had to use a horse switch to get them to move. This time when I trotted down the highway, I think I saw fingers. I often wonder if dad got those mules in retaliation, or if he actually had my best interest at heart. Either way, it worked out for me.

CHAPTER 26

It seemed peculiar when we started work on the new farm. So few of us left and a war raging on, but a positive side to all this was that we lucked out when the beet thinning and the beet topping rolled around. Idaho had built a prisoner of war camp in Paul, very near to where our farm was located. I don't know how any of this worked out from a legal standpoint, but during these harvest times, the farmers would bring in alot of these prisoners of war to work the crops. They brought them in army trucks with guards everywhere, stationed at the ends of the fields, with rifles slung over their shoulders. I never saw any bayonets, and believe me I was looking out for them. We were afraid at first, working right alongside all these prisoners, but soon realized that they were just a lonely bunch of boys, some of them were very young, away from their homeland and families. We weren't allowed to talk to them, too much, but dad had a field day talking German with some of them and actually became such good friends with a couple of them, that they moved to Rupert after the war, bringing their families and stayed friends till the end.

As if we didn't have enough work loaded on us all the time, dad accepted five newborn lambs from a sheepherder, who came to the door, peddling baby lambs to anyone that would take care of them because their mother ewes had rejected them. Hildegard and I were given the extra chore of having to get up in the middle of the night and go out to the barn and feed them their milk from Pepsi bottles, with a big rubber nipple on it. Needless to say, we really got attached to them and they to us, as they grew up, we would run and play with them. One day we came home from school and we didn't see them anywhere around, then we found out that dad had taken them to the stockyard and sold all five of them. That day Hildegard and I went into temper tantrums in front of dad and I can still see the look on his face, as he handed each of us a five dollar bill. That took care of the tears real fast.

CHAPTER 27

The one thing we always welcomed were Sundays off, a day of well needed rest. Our parents never veered from that one bit, if they could help it. It hadn't taken dad very long to find us another church to attend as soon as we arrived from North Dakota. It was a lot easier getting to church now and we all really enjoyed it. Hildegard and I sang in the choir for many years, we also belonged to the youth organization where we met some lifelong friends there. Many times we would bring some friends home and our parents seemed to love it. They would laugh and joke with them and make them feel right at home. So we weren't surprised when dad allowed a soldier, a first cousin of ours, to spend his entire two week furlough at our house, from the army. During that time, one Saturday evening, mother had some urgent material that needed to be delivered to the church before the Sunday morning service, so she asked this soldier guest if he would drive me to get this delivered to the church. So we drove to the church and made the delivery as instructed and headed for home.

We were driving along, when suddenly this soldier turned off of the main highway and started to drive down a dark narrow dirt road, to nowhere. I questioned his turning off of the highway and without saying a word; he pulled over, stopped the car, turned off the headlights being pitch dark by now. He came to the passenger side where I was sitting, opened the door and quickly grabbed hold of me. I was totally shocked when he then slammed me across the front bench seat of the car, and I started to fight back with all my strength, but within seconds he had complete control of me, he stretched my arms over my head, then he pinned me under the steering wheel, and proceeded to rape me. I was struggling and crying and he kept saying, "It's okay, it's okay"! After which he got back into the car and proceeded to drive home, without saying one word and I was definitely speechless myself. Still crying and shaking, I was so happy when he pulled into our yard; before he came to a full stop I jumped out of the car and ran into the house, going straight upstairs to go to bed. As close as Hildegard and I had always been, I couldn't bring myself to tell her, but what to tell when I wasn't sure what had actually happened to me. When I saw that my under panties were stained with blood, I panicked even more. I knew that I couldn't put them in the laundry basket for fear that mother might ask questions. So my decision was to sneak them to the farm with me where I walked to a far corner of one of the fields, dug a deep hole at a spot that I knew would never be plowed up and there I buried my secret, for the next sixty five years.

That soldier rat had the nerve to keep hanging around our house for the last few days of his furlough. I was busy keeping my distance, as I loathed him. He never apologized or seemed to have any remorse about what he had put me through.

As soon as he left and was out of my sight, I felt a lot of relief but felt in need to talk to someone. I decided that God would be my counselor, so I took all my woes to him in prayer and ultimately felt some relief of the turmoil going on inside me. It took a very long time, but, time heals.

I struggled to stay on track in school. I wanted to stick my head in the books and study and study and study. Hildegard and I were never able to join any of the extra-curricular school activities that might have taken my mind off of things, and we were always needed at home, the minute school let out we had to go home. Our folks never stopped us from going to high school, but they didn't do a whole lot to support us either. Every year on registration day, we had to plead with dad for the seven dollars we needed for books. They paid no attention when we stayed home from school anytime we wanted to. When we wanted to stay home, we would just write our own excuse slips the next morning and mother would always sign them without reading what it said. We packed our own lunches every morning and at lunchtime, a lot of the other kids, would run to town and buy hamburgers and Pepsi colas then sit and eat in the park, while Hildegard and I sat there eating our peanut butter and dark karo syrup sandwiches and drink water from the fountain, all the while, the intoxicating aroma from the hamburgers wafted past our noses. We never got hamburgers. One school morning, for some reason or other, Hildegard and I decided to skip school, but we didn't want to stay home, because they always found something for us to do and we were ready for a day of leisure, so we went and sat under a dry canal bridge, so we couldn't be seen. We had a great time just chatting and finally talked ourselves into quitting school. We decided if we quit then and there we would get a small refund for our books and then we could go to town and buy us one of them hamburgers and maybe even a Pepsi cola. That sealed the deal!! We left our peanut butter and syrup sandwiches under the bridge and ran to school as fast as our legs carried us. We went straight to the principal's office and promptly quit school. No one there tried to talk us out of it, especially with only four weeks of school left for the entire year and finals right around the corner. They just looked at us as if we were crazy. The paperwork now finished and the small refund in our hands; we ran to town and bought us one of those hamburgers and a Pepsi cola, then scarfed them down. We walked home but never told our parents what we had done, of course they had no idea why we'd come home early and we knew that, but we weren't so lucky when our brother Ted found out about it a few days later and he gave us a lecture we didn't soon forget. He raved about the importance of an education that he never had a chance at. He said he would personally show up the next fall and drag our butts back to school come hell or high water. He did just that!! He made us register that fall but we were ignorant of the fact that we didn't need to take the first semester over again because we had successfully passed all that already. No one there informed us otherwise and in our ignorance we registered to take over my entire junior year and Hildegard's entire sophomore year. All the principal ever said to us was, "I hope you stay this time!!" Today I look at it as four years of high school and one year of college. Besides which, I still think it was all worth that delicious hamburger and Pepsi cola we could finally have.

At the beginning of my senior year, dad sold our forty acre farm to my brothers. I was never happier to finally be able to hang up my overalls and I haven't worn anything that has a bib since, not even an apron. Dad had always told us, "As long as you stick your feet under my dining table, you must work." I decided the time had come for me to start thinking about owning my own dining table on which to stick my feet under. In a pinch, we were still required to help our brothers on the farm, dad developed a hobby of raising pigs, he always loved his pigs, he built pen after pen, then he'd buy and sell hogs at the local stockyard. He raised a lot of corn, to feed them, on his twelve acres he still had in town. He seemed so involved with those pigs, I was afraid he was going to start sleeping with them.

He was very happy and content. I had watched this man working like no other for so many years, that it was gratifying to see him relax and enjoy his life, smiling much more often. Mother was also more relaxed and finally had the privilege of enjoying an electric stove, automatic washer and dryer, some modern appliances; and she got a lot more rest, but unfortunately, she developed some health problems, surgeries, diabetes, mini strokes. There was never such a thing as medical insurance, at least not in our family. When mother was in need of major surgery, dad went to the bank to borrow the money for medical bills. The banker asked how he intended to pay it back. My father said, "I raise pigs, I feed them, then they go lay in the shade and I go lay in the shade. When they grow up, I sell them and pay you back. The bank loaned him the money and that's exactly how he paid them back. She sadly passed away at the young age of sixty five, after another one of her many strokes. Dad did remarry, but also lost that wife and stayed a bachelor till he passed away at age eighty six.

CHAPTER 28

My senior year was beginning to open up a whole new world for me. I had learned a lot by now and hopefully was somewhat wiser. Hildegard and I were finally able to attend ball games, pep rallies after school and I even played basketball for awhile and I actually enjoyed and was fairly good at it. After years of slinging potatoes, sugar beets, hay, manure, mud, you name it, I had no problem slinging a basketball. But the one thing I had always wanted to do was to play in the school band, so I registered to take band, but my parents wouldn't furnish me with an instrument, so the band teacher didn't know what else to do with me but hand me two huge brass cymbals which I had to clang together at the precise moment. I didn't care, I was happy to be where I'd always wanted to be, which was one of the band members at a ball game. When we played, I was stuck in the rear, intensely staring at my music sheet so as not to miss my cue at that precise moment when I had to clang the cymbals; which I did with all my strength so you can be sure I was heard, as I proudly looked out into the bleachers to make sure that everyone noticed me.

I always called Hildegard my "sidekick" cause we were always side by side. We worked together, laughed together, we cried together, we fought together, we played together, and we still like being together. We both happen to be red heads and mother even dressed us alike, and people always thought we were twins. One day we heard that the four lane bowling alley in town was looking for pin setters, actually as we learned later, they were always looking for pin setters, nobody stayed with that job for very long, but we were ready for some real labor again, we were getting rusty and a little money of our own wouldn't hurt either. We rushed to the bowling alley and applied and were hired on the spot. We were to start work immediately. Our hours were from 7:00p.m. to closing time at 1:00a.m. We were paid fifteen cents per lane for every lane that was bowled. Our job was to set up the bowling pins in their proper fashion after they had been knocked over. We had to sit on a very narrow ledge and as soon as the bowler knocked over the pins, we'd jump from the ledge and hurriedly gather the pins and place them in a huge tray overhead, working as fast as we could to make it back on the ledge before the next ball came crashing down. Again the rest of the pins were then picked up, we filled the tray, and then we slowly lowered this tray, which was now loaded with swaying pins that we had to control so as not to knock over the still standing ones, all the while, the impatient bowlers were yelling obscenities at us for not being fast enough. No doubt we were used to work, but here we were using muscles we never knew we had. Not only could we hardly get out of bed the next morning, but we were black and blue from the flying pins hitting us everywhere. Hildegard would say, "At least now we get paid for our black and blue marks!" At 1:00a.m. , we walked home in the pitch dark of night. We always walked to and from work. I get the shivers yet, when I think of the soldiers from the camp milling around town, sometimes they would even walk us home. The honest truth is not one soldier ever made a pass at us, as we talked and laughed. I'm assuming that they were just a bunch of young lonely boys away from home and enjoyed our company. I don't know how long we worked setting pins, but we finally quit. Ducking bowling pins wasn't exactly what I had in mind for the rest of my life.

Hildegard and I started going to the Saturday night dances at the Rat Race Dancehall in Burley which had a country western band called the "Happy

Five". Wow!! We were beginning to have some real fun. There was never a shortage of guys to dance with, having all those soldiers around, and believe me, we never turned down a single one either. We were fast learners and we danced the Jitterbug till our feet fell off! Hildegard found herself a boyfriend before I did, he was a nice local boy from our church, but now we had a problem. With mother sticking to the old custom ways, that girls should always marry from the eldest on down to the youngest, which then meant we had to have boyfriends in that order also. Since I was the older one, we needed to get our heads together and come up with a plan; a plan where we had to clue in her boyfriend for this plan to work. We knew that mom would be spying on us, so when her boyfriend came to pick us up, I was to slide in the front seat and sit next to Hildegard's boyfriend, while she climbed in the back seat, but only till we barely got out of the yard, before Hildegard was already jealous, and we had to stop so we could trade places. It got worse! When he brought us home from the dance, heaven forbid if we didn't walk in the house together, mother always slept with one eye open. We then came up with another plan, that when we got home from the dance, I would only go in the house as far as the front porch, then I would sit under piles of overcoats and sweaters hanging there, to keep from freezing to death, while I waited for them to finish their "necking" (that's what we called love making in those days) while they were sitting in a nice warm car. When Hildegard was ready, we would walk in the house together. I call that true sibling dedication!! One evening at this dance, a soldier asked to take me home, but I was saved by the bell when he asked if it was okay with me that he was riding with another couple. I felt safer and accepted. We got to my house, parked in the yard and we started hugging and kissing, as was the couple in the front seat. I didn't last long because this guy reached down my blouse and got rough with my boobies; I slapped his face got out of the car and ran in the house. Hadn't the preacher always said, "Don't sin or you'll go to hell and burn forever"? Word must have got around the camp because not another soldier ever asked me out, but they would still ask me to dance.

I was doing surprisingly well in school, physics and math being my favorite subjects. I was taken aback one day when my physics teacher, Mr. Bromenschenkel, asked me what my plans were after high school graduation. What plans? I had no idea, till he said to me, "You have been pulling such good grades, maybe you should consider college." That was something I'd heard about, but the farthest thing from my mind, up till then. I was physically stirred to tears, that someone cared what I did with my future, and I did what he said, I started to think about it and came to the conclusion that I couldn't just go off to a college without some help and support from my parents, of which I was pretty sure I'd never receive. I finally mustered up enough courage to try one day, when dad was in a good mood, I just blurted out, "Dad, I want to go to college!" He looked at me for a second and then he waved his big hand in the air and said, "Go!!" He said nothing more, but I finished it off with the question, "Could I depend on some help?" Then and there the discussion ended as fast as it had begun, as I had expected, not much disappointment there, so I put that all behind me and started to look ahead. Since I was raised in the farming business all my life, and I'd had enough of that, there weren't a lot of choices for a career in a small town, so a lot of my friends went to work at the local Simplot potato factory, but I really didn't want to look at any more potatoes.

Finding jobs being somewhat limited, as was entertainment other than going to a movie or go bowling. But there were a lot of beautiful mountains, rivers and lakes all around, so it was a great place for fishing and hunting. Going to the mountains to fish for salmon, in the ice cold Snake River stream, was great fun, that is, for most people. Personally, I was never cut out to be a fisherman, and worse yet, I detested camping in a make-shift tent, sleeping in a sleeping bag, on the bare ground, waking up in the morning and see a big tarantula sleeping next to your pillow, even worse was having to go to the bathroom in the bushes, where the snakes hissed at your bare butt, I'm not so sure that anybody else was as crazy about it as they let on, because they all have nice modernized camper trailers and motor homes, which they use today. That seems to me like dragging my housework with me, making beds, cleaning up, cooking meals, I don't see that as a get-a-way from the everyday doldrums.

I must say though, there is a positive side to roughing it. There is nothing like eating a meal of fresh cooked salmon that had just been pulled out of the river, gutted, and stuffed with loads of butter, onions, and garlic wrapped in tin foil, tossed and cooked in an open fire pit. The side dish was equally as delicious, using a large cast iron pot, filled to the brim with fresh sliced Idaho potatoes, layered with pounds of butter, sliced onions, then covered with beer then setting the pot onto an open fire pit, and savor the aroma of the sizzling butter and beer, boiling over into this fire pit. A meal that is impossible to match in one's own kitchen.

As I was keeping my eyes wide open, I noticed a new building being built across from the bowling alley, where I'd once worked. I saw some workers milling around so I decided to walk over to see what it was they were building. This fellow who was bending down doing something or other, stood up and looked at me so I asked what it was they were building. He replied, "We are building a restaurant; drive-in." I said, "I'm graduating soon and I'm looking for a job, but I don't know anything about being a waitress." He told me to fill out an application and it asked for previous experience, I just put "farming." I didn't put the setting up of bowling pins. I handed in the application and left without asking this fellow's name. I went back to cramming for finals and my long awaited graduation. Then one day shortly before graduation day, my girlfriend Lucille came up to me, very excited and told me that she had found a job in Burley, as a secretary and wanted to know if I would be interested in finding work there and share an apartment with her. That sounded like a plan and I had nothing else going for me, so I went job hunting in Burley and was soon hired at the downtown five and ten cent store called, "Kings". Lucille already had some help from her parents who had given her an old car, well that was more than I had, still riding our three wheel bicycle. I had a lot of reservations and mixed emotions, but I decided it was a beginning. So I agreed to go. Graduation day was in the month of May 1947. I was floating on cloud nine; my parents had even paid to rent my cap and gown. I had never felt so happy and elated in my entire life, as I did at that moment, when I was handed this beautiful purple and gold (school colors) diploma. I clutched it to my chest as if to never let it go, and I didn't, I still have it today in mint condition. Now it was time for the move to Burley, which wouldn't take long, I didn't need a truck with what few possessions I had, I could take on a bicycle. I had been putting off telling my parents anything of my plans of moving to Burley and time was running out. So one evening, I told them what I was about to do; that I was moving to

Burley immediately. The reaction I got from both my parents was no more than if I would've said to them, "I'm going to the bathroom now." Then I thought, at least they didn't say no! The next morning, I went upstairs to pack my total worth into a small suitcase mother let me use. She happened to be sitting at her new noisy weaving loom, weaving rugs, which was her hobby at the time and all you could hear was "Bam squeak, bam squeak". For a split second I almost wished that I could just go out to the barn, harness up the mules and head down the highway to the farm, not a worry in the world. I soon came to my senses to hurry up. Lucille was already waiting to take me to the apartment that she had already rented, but I hadn't seen yet. I finally picked up the packed little suitcase, walked past mother at the loom, which never faltered to the rhythm, "Bam squeak, bam squeak", but she did look up at me with this faint smile on her face, I smiled back and disappeared down the stairs and out the door I went. I jumped into Lucille's car and we drove out the driveway onto the highway to Burley and into the sunset of the unknown and very hopefully a new life, I thought!!! It wasn't long when Lucille pulled up to this red brick house near town, she walked me around the outside of the house, down a few crooked, cracked cement steps, to a door with four locks on it that opened to a basement apartment that Lucille had rented from an older couple that lived in the house upstairs. I was already a little nauseated from walking out of my home, but the sight of my future home almost finished me off. My first thought was that it looked like an oversized jail cell. Just one big room, a couple of small rugs on the cement floor, one double bed on which we would both sleep, a hole in the wall to hang a few clothes, the bathroom was just an alcove, that had a curtain you could pull across for privacy. There was no kitchen per say, just a small table holding a two burner hot plate, on which to cook our meals. The place was damp and dark with just one small lamp for light and a very small narrow oblong window, directly above the small table, which let in very little light, due to the tall lawn grass, just outside. I swallowed my disappointment and said little. I was now at the mercy of Lucille till I would start earning my own paycheck to do my share. No turning back now! Lying in bed that first night, my brain worked overtime, as I was thinking that my life as a young girl had all started in an attic, and after all those years of toil and sweat, I've ended up in a basement, it didn't seem that I'd been very successful in working my way up. After a sleepless night, I got ready and walked to work that morning. And every morning for that matter.

At my new job, they started me out, sneaking around the store all day, acting like I was dusting and straightening up, but in actuality, I was to keep my eyes on customers to see if they were stealing anything. Boring!!! Then I was promoted to stocking shelves. I didn't like my job very much, but I had made my bed, so now I had to sleep in it. One late evening, Lucille's boyfriend, who had decided to stop in totally unannounced, knocked on our door. We were startled and I yelled, "Who's there?" He didn't answer, I suspect he sensed the urgency in my voice, (I was always spooky anyway) he then must have decided to play a trick on us, so he pounded hard on the door, and this time Lucille yelled, "Who's there?" The man in a gruff voice then threatened to break down the door unless we opened it pronto. I wasn't going to mess with this any longer and I wasted not another minute, so in less than thirty seconds I jumped on the top of the little table and knocked out that entire little

basement window with my bare hands, I crawled
out, I ran across the yard and jumped a six foot
hedge then went running down the street, before I
finally looked back and saw that Lucille was no
more than ten feet behind me. After the fact, the
boyfriend was doubled over with laughter, but after
I got a few kicks in, he had another reason to
double over, but not with laughter this time. We
were really frightened out of our wits and when we
went to go to bed I said to Lucille, "I want to go
back home!" I was totally surprised when she
replied, "Me too!" I couldn't help but chuckle,
thinking one chicken, maybe, two chickens, it's best
we go home! Our first priority the next morning
was to go upstairs and face the landlord to explain.
This old couple sat there with their mouths hanging
to the floor as we explained the scenario that had
happened the night before, we offered to pay to
have the window replaced, but they wouldn't hear
of it, maybe they thought we were a couple of
crazies and couldn't wait to get us out the door.

The next morning, we didn't even give notice at
work; we just packed up our few belongings and
headed back to Rupert. Lucille dropped me off at
our house, I walked in, clutching the little suitcase
and I started up the stairs only to hear the familiar

beat of the loom, "Bam squeak, bam squeak". Then I thought it seems like I had just done this not so long ago, only in complete reverse. As I reached the top of the stairs, mother looked over at me, with a much bigger grin this time, which read like a book, she needn't have said a word. Believe me, it never felt so good to be able to stick my feet under dad's dining table once again.

I soon put the whole sad experience behind me, because I already knew what my next move would be, and that was going back to this new building that was being built, which was now up and running and was called "Cooper's Drive-Inn", a combination of a restaurant with curbside service. When I got there, I saw this same man I had talked to earlier who had taken my application. I learned that his name was Boyd Cooper, the owner. He looked surprised to see me and said, "Where have you been?" I said, "Don't ask!" I told him that I was still looking for a job and without a minute's hesitation he said, rather sternly, "Go home and get yourself a white uniform and be back here to work tomorrow at 4:00p.m., sharp". I was taken aback for a second, but just for a second because I was thinking, "I'm gonna get along great with this boss, he sounds too much like my father". The next day, wearing my white uniform, I walked to work at this place called "Cooper's Drive-Inn"! I knew nothing about being a waitress, but I knew how to run around and wait on all those cars parked outside, slinging hamburgers. I wasn't quite as chipper inside the restaurant at the soda fountain. This place was very busy from the get go which didn't leave much time for training, so I was left to flounder as best I could. The very first customer I had was a lady and her two children that came in and were seated at the counter. As I waited on them, the lady ordered three cherry cokes. We'd always been told that a coke was merely a soft drink, which was a big drawback for me. So when she said cherry cokes, I thought, oh that's easy enough, so I filled three glasses with ice, I squirted some cherry syrup into each one and filled them with carbonated water, then I set these three red drinks in front of these people. She never said one word to me, they drank them and left. Not until later did I realize my mistake. My boss, Boyd, never knew about this, but he will now if he happens to read this book. There was only one other problem I had, the town piano teacher, a nice looking sophisticated lady, came in for dinner one evening, I waited on her and she ordered a T-bone steak. As I served it to her, I heard her mumble something about the letter A. I had no idea what she was mumbling about so I nonchalantly ignored her, she called me over a second time and again mumbled A-something. I thought she was talking about grades when I finally went to the cook and said she wants an A-something. He picked up the bottle of A-1 sauce and handed it to me, so I gave it to the lady. Before that, I had never even heard of a T-bone steak, let alone anything about any A-1 sauce. Another lesson learned. I loved my job and I worked hard at it and I learned fast. One day my boss, Boyd, came up to me and said, "You are a good fast worker, do you have any sisters I could hire?" Well, having six sisters I said, "Sure, how many do you need?" He did hire Hildegard and I was elated to have my sidekick back. Later, Ella was also hired. By now I had eaten and looked at so many hamburgers, I almost got sick of them and wondered what ever possessed me to quit high school for one of them. I really loved my job and all the customers. I was still naïve and had an awful lot to learn from being thrown into this very public atmosphere. This drive-in happened to be located directly across the way from the local freight and passenger train depot, so we got the gang of regular train engineers for breakfast, every single morning, very early. They were a rough looking bunch of guys and they relished in teasing me, "this young red-headed, green eyed, naïve little girl," just to watch me blush a beet red. They constantly played the song on the jukebox with the lyrics that said, "I've got a gal with red hair and green eyes, I love her and I know she loves me!" I'd go blushing to their utmost satisfaction, but I kept on working and ignored them.

One day, a regular handsome fellow customer took a liking to me and finally asked me for a date. I was nineteen years old and definitely ready for a boyfriend, so we started dating. He was a perfect gentleman in every way. He respected me, holding me tight, kissing me so gently, caressing me outside of my clothes, I loved his kisses, I couldn't get enough of him kissing me. I don't know if he was that good or if I was that bad. He started talking marriage way too early in the relationship. I panicked and I knew he was everything a girl could ever want, except for me, he was a career farmer. Now I have nothing against farmers, but I had visions of having to go back to the hard life I had just escaped from. After some serious soul searching, I reluctantly broke up with him never giving it a thought that I might have been a sweetheart rather than just a hard working farmer's wife. He didn't take it very well. But I went on with my life and I hope he did too. Cooper's Drive-Inn was basically a family business and about the same time I'd broken up with my boyfriend, my boss, Boyd's, brother Miles, who was a cook at the drive-in, had also broken up with his girlfriend. He was a tall, handsome, outgoing fun guy to be around and I soon had my eyes on him, and he obviously had his eyes on me, because it wasn't too long before he asked me for a date. We hit it off from the very beginning; we had so much fun together. It all seemed so natural. Those of us who worked the night shift used to go, what we called, "hooky-bobbin", "sledding" after closing the restaurant at 1:00a.m. We would all pile on this big sled, and thread a heavy rope through the rear bumper of someone's automobile, who would then pull us down the open highway; there was no traffic at that time of night. Someone would use this rope to whip the sled back and forth over the icy roads flying into one barrow pit, up across the highway and into the other barrow pit, sometimes we missed a telephone pole by a mere inch; we were very lucky that we never had a single casualty, other than someone flying of the sled and land head first in a snow bank, legs kicking in the air for help. Many times we would go back to the drive-in afterwards and eat hot chili. The night cops, who we knew well, usually looked the other way. In the summertime, we would do a similar thing, going water skiing, again being dragged down the water canal bank with a rope on the bumper of a car with one person riding on a homemade water board.

CHAPTER 29

I was still allowed to live at home. That was the noble thing that our parents always did, they allowed any one of us to live at home as long as we needed to, never kicked a one of us out, yet, they let us flounder to find our own way, there was no direction on their part about our futures'. When I left for a short time to go to Burley, they never asked me why I left, they never asked me why I came back, and they never asked me where I was going, but they allowed me to live at home, no questions asked. I loved my job at the drive-in, Miles and I had so much fun together, I didn't think life could get any better, so when Miles asked me to marry him very early in our relationship, I didn't hesitate to accept, and soon wedding plans were in order. On September 28, 1947, we were married in a beautiful ceremony at my church, followed by a great reception at the Rat Race Dancehall in Burley, dancing to the "Happy Five Band", lots of beer and snacks. In order to afford such a lavish celebration, the trend for most weddings in the community at the time, was that, at the reception, the wedding cake was auctioned off, slice by slice, each slice being held up for bidding where buyers would bid anywhere from one dollar a slice to as high as twenty five dollars a slice. Proceeds usually covered expenses, plus, everybody had a great time, even some walk-ins would join the fun. Miles and I drove to Salt Lake City for a short honeymoon, then back to the real world to start a whole new life. We were raised and taught that marriage is sacred and forever, and it's the wife's duty to take care of her husband and family. There was no such thing as birth control pills at that time; the only thing available was what they called a diaphragm, which required a doctor's visit for the fitting and instruction of its use. I did everything I was supposed to do but I don't think mine worked, because every time I sneezed, it popped out. No surprise there that I soon became pregnant, I was still scarfing down those hamburgers and ended up gaining sixty pounds. I stayed on at work until the end of my pregnancy so now when those train engineers came in for breakfast, they were playing a new song on the jukebox with the lyrics, "I don't want her, you can have her, she's too fat for me!"

CHAPTER 30

On August 11, 1948, our first daughter, Eunice, was born, weighing in at 10lbs. 6oz. My mother offered to take care of our baby, so I went back to work. Miles had never liked being a cook at the restaurant, so he decided to pursue his dream, to be a butcher at a supermarket meat department. He took the required six week course and was soon hired at a local market. His boss, Joe, happened to be an avid archer, and he soon had Miles interested in joining the local archery club. It also interested me enough to join with him, so we each purchased our own bow and arrows and went target shooting on our days off. We both loved the sport, but Miles took it a step further, where he and his boss would go hunting for live game. So when open deer hunting season came around, they would take off for the hills with their bows and arrows, and one year, to everyone's surprise, Miles shot a huge antlered buck with his bow and arrow and became the town celebrity for awhile. He was even featured on the front cover of the National Archery magazine that month. There was a lot of meat on that buck and I personally didn't care for venison, so I saved some choice steaks for Miles and ground up the rest of this deer into hamburger meat, then I went to the local, self-help cannery, and canned one hundred 28 ounce cans of venison chili with beans and they come in mighty handy one day as you'll read about, later in this book. Miles also had this deer head mounted and it still hangs in my daughter's living room.

By now, Miles and I had moved from our apartment to a three bedroom house we rented close to where we worked. Life was good until one day, Boyd surprised us with the news that he would be leaving Rupert to pursue his lifelong dream of becoming a medical doctor and that his sister and brother-in-law, Mike and Marion, would be the new owners of the drive-in. We were sad to see him go; I stayed on at work and was pregnant with my second child. Just by chance, one day, Miles and I were driving by this quaint little two bedroom house that had a "For Sale" sign, it had a white picket fence surrounding a plush green lawn. It was so inviting that in the fall of 1951, we bought it for $1,400.00. We were now proud homeowners when our second daughter, Marilyn, was born on June 12, 1952. By now, I was only working part time. Life was a blast, all settled, two healthy children, good jobs, and we owned our own home. I felt like I had finally arrived and life would be a bowl of cherries. Then the bombshell!!

CHAPTER 31

We got news that the drive-in was up for sale and Miles' entire family would be moving to Southern California, where the sun always shines and it never snows. With my mouth hanging open, I don't know if I was hearing right when they asked if Miles and I were interested in purchasing the drive-in or did we want to make the move to California with the rest of the family. My mind went spinning again – I knew that this drive-in was a very lucrative business, that is, if you were willing to work day and night. What a heart rending decision, on which way to swing the pendulum. Miles did not like being a cook for the rest of his life; he loved his job in the meat business, so we opted to move to California with the rest of the family, lock, stock, and barrel. My emotions were wearing thin by now. I had only heard good things about California, but I would have to leave behind my parents, my brothers and sisters, whom I'd lived around my whole life and they weren't too happy to see me leave either. But the preparations began!!

First of all, I was terribly concerned on how we were going to afford all this; we had been living paycheck to paycheck, no savings to speak of. Mike and Marion were the first to leave for California and were very supportive in allowing us to throw a few of our belongings on to their truck. We wrapped up some last minute business necessities and finally, Miles tied Marilyn's crib onto the roof of our 1948 Pontiac, we piled all of our clothes in the back seat of the car, the trunk was filled up with the 100 cans of venison chili, we said our goodbyes, and in February 1953, we headed for this place called California. I tried to be brave and excited, but was sick to my stomach at the same time. There was no job waiting for us, no house to live in, but then I thought, "We can always sleep on a park bench and eat cold venison chili till we get back on our feet." As sad as I was when we left Rupert, my tears dried real fast as soon as we entered California. Flowers everywhere, palm trees lining the streets, the sun shining brightly, soothing warm weather beating down on us, I looked at Miles and said, "I think we made the right decision", with a big grin on his face he agreed. Mike and Marion were so kind to have had already rented an apartment for us which we were able to occupy immediately, in the city of Inglewood, California, near where they themselves were now living and where Miles parents also lived.

By coincidence, our apartment happened to be located directly across the street from the Hollywood race track. I thought, "Can I ever get away from those darn horses!" One thing was for sure, I would never bet on one.

CHAPTER 32

Miles went job hunting immediately, and with his experience as a butcher, he was able to find work rather quickly at a major supermarket. We were still eating venison chili for breakfast, lunch and dinner, till he was able to bring home some real steaks. I was beginning to really enjoy looking at that mounted deer head that was hanging on our living room wall.

The apartment was small and I soon needed to scout for a bigger place for us to live and found a three bedroom Spanish stucco house in a very nice neighborhood and the rent was affordable, but the place had been left a total pig sty by the previous renters to the point that it was literally nauseating. I told the landlord, a nice older gentleman, that I was willing to clean it up, and totally paint it, if he would furnish me all the paint I needed. To my surprise, he hesitated. I wanted the house and I tried to convince him that in no way could he ever rent it in that condition. He finally agreed to buy me all the paint I needed. I had a mountain of work ahead of me, seemed like I was always facing too much work and not enough play. I bought gallons of snow white paint and a couple of 4" brushes, no paint rollers yet, and went to work. The first thing I did was tear down and discard every filthy and torn pull shade on all the windows that were truly unsalvageable. I painted every room this snow white, ceilings, cabinets, inside and out, second coats needed in many places, then I ended by polishing all the hardwood floors to a glistening shine. I called the landlord and informed him that I needed new window shades. He became very angry when I told him that I had to throw them all away. He came rushing over, I suppose to give me a piece of his mind, till he walked in, I nearly needed to pick him off the floor. He looked around and finally said, "Order all the window shades you need!" Then he totally surprised me by giving me a 9x12 area rug and an upholstered couch for the living room.

CHAPTER 33

My brother-in-law Mike was working for a water company called Sparkletts, delivering five gallon bottles of drinking water to homes and merchants and doing so well that Miles decided to change jobs and go to work for Sparkletts also, where he would have much better working conditions and better hours having all weekends off and much better pay. It was a lucrative move! He loved working for Sparkletts and stayed on for the next thirty years at which time, he retired. I was very happy, since it allowed me to be a stay at home mom.

What a great experience for me when I saw the ocean for the first time. We spent many weekends at the beautiful beaches where the kids loved playing in the sand. We actually used to go and play in the sand dunes, what is now LAX. I still have videos of that. The Sparkletts plant was located in Long Beach, so Miles was driving it every day, which left me without a car where I needed to walk Eunice to school every morning, where she had started kindergarten, I also needed to carry Marilyn, because she was only one year old. Having no stroller, my problem was solved one day when

Miles and I were driving down the road and happened to see this model - A Ford automobile sitting by the side of the road with a sign in the window that said "For Sale - $25.00" and a phone number. I said to Miles, "I think we could afford that as a second car." We called the fellow and we promptly gave him a check and drove the model - A Ford home. I drove it everywhere, I got a few looks, but it took me where I wanted to go, I even enjoyed having to crank it to get it started.

One day I got a phone call from Marion, in a panic, telling me she had just realized that she had a lot of green stamps (which we collected at the time) and they were to expire that very day and would I please drive her to downtown L.A. to redeem them. She knew that all I had was the model –A but she was desperate, so I said yes and we took the children and drove off to Los Angeles. We made it there alright and she was able to get the backyard barbecue she wanted, but it was so large that we had to take it out of its box to even fit it in the rumble seat. This motor in the model – A ran very loud, but we chugged along home, Cadillacs and BMW's passing us up left and right, looking over at us as if we were something out of "The Grapes of

Wrath"!   A little embarrassing, but mission accomplished.

Rather than make the drive to work every day, Miles and I decided to move to Long Beach. This time we rented a nice clean three bedroom house. Eunice was starting first grade that year. Long Beach was a nice city, beautiful beaches and we liked living there a lot, but we didn't live there that long, because we decided that California had been good to us and we knew that we were here to stay. We went house hunting to buy our own home again; we found a new tract of houses being built high up in the hills, in the city of Torrance, which was about halfway between Inglewood and Long Beach and very close to most beaches along the ocean, from Long Beach to Redondo Beach to Malibu Beach. We purchased a three bedroom, two bath home for $14,500.00. It had a large bay window with a panoramic view from Redondo Beach to San Pedro, where all the lights at night were a beautiful sight and the Goodyear blimp floating by every day. The children loved that. We sold our house in Rupert for $2,500.00 and bought ourselves a brand new Pontiac automobile.

About the same time we moved to our new home, the new Disneyland Park in Anaheim also had its grand opening. So we took the children and really enjoyed this happy wonderland. We returned there often because it was such a fun place. Then, one day I got the surprise of my life; I received word that my parents were coming to visit us, I could hardly believe it, and I was so overjoyed. I picked them up at the train depot in downtown L.A. and they were shocked by all the traffic. They were even more shocked the day I took them to see the ocean for the first time ever! The morning we were all ready to go, dad came out of the bedroom wearing his suit, tie, hat, and black polished shoes. I gasped and said, "Dad, we are going to the beach! "I soon realized that whenever our dad went somewhere, he always wore his suit. I never saw my dad wear a sport coat or dress pants or even a sweater; it was either overalls or his suit. Mother had dressed up as well. Needless to say, I couldn't take them any farther than the boardwalk. For me to be able to see their faces as they stared at this vast ocean, for the very first time, was mind boggling. Dad stared out into the horizon, and then said, "That's China over there!" I got happy tears in my eyes, to think that little old me could give them such pleasure and joy, which I never thought possible. My head was swelling with pride in how much I really loved them. Then I drove them around to let them see the acres and acres of orange groves, they oohed and aahed with excitement. I couldn't help but commit a faux pas and pull over to the side of the road and pick a couple of oranges off a tree limb that was drooping over the fence. I handed them each an orange and they looked at them like, "Oh is that where they come from?" Being a farmer, I'm sure dad already had a good idea, but it was the moment!! I'm wondering if they had mixed feelings back then, when I moved away from Idaho and they wanted to see for themselves how I fared, for their own peace of mind. I'd like to think they went home with good feelings and maybe even pleasantly surprised. I think it was one of the highlights of my life and maybe theirs also.

Chapter 34

We loved our new home, we had wonderful neighbors, having parties, what more could anyone ask for, I thought!! Miles kept reminding me that we never had the son he always pined for, our daughters were now nine and five years old when he brought it up again, I finally said to him, "if I have to have another baby, we better get started tonight, because I'm almost 30 years old already. Nine months later on December 31, 1957, our third daughter, Annette was born on New Year's Eve, at 11:50 p.m. at the Torrance memorial hospital. When Miles was told that he another daughter, he said, "I guess it's time for the big V ", I said, Oh good, a vasectomy", he replied" no, I was thinking of buying a big van". This was now the second time in my life I made the local newspaper, because, Annette was the last baby born, in the city of Torrance, in the year 1957. Life was good and I soon became an even busier stay at home mom. Eunice and Marilyn were both attending the parochial school at the church we belonged to, and where I'd been a room mother, I taught Sunday school, I sang in the choir, I worked with the youth group; I had been an officer of the women's group, called the Mary Martha Society. I even helped the trusties of the church paint the school and church room. In between all this time, my mother-in-law, had opened her own fabric store business, and whenever she was in need of some extra help, she would call on me. That opened a whole new world for me. I became so involved in what her customers were sewing for their families; I became determined to do the same for my own family. I purchased a sewing machine, got some fabrics and patterns, and began to spend all my spare time following the instructions of these patterns in every detail. I was a fast learner, and it wasn't too long before my girls were the best dressed kids in school. Later on, I did go for more advanced tailoring classes and actually became a professional seamstress, where I was sewing garments for fashion shows for the local fabric stores. I also had a clientele of my own, doing custom sewing out of my home for extra income. I was truly in my element and loved every minute of it. It was soon time for me to have a better car to chase around in, so we purchased a used, Renault, a small French made automobile. I was out driving one day, I was approaching one of the busiest intersections in

Torrance, (Crenshaw and Pacific Coast Hwy) I had the green light, I proceeded to go through when my Renault totally died, smack in the center of the intersection, cars stopped all around me, I could not get the Renault started, no matter what I did, I had no other choice but to get out and push it off the road. (I had forgotten that sometime earlier, I must have unbuttoned my slacks at the waist, possibly of some discomfort or other) by now the light had turned red for me and I'm still sitting in the middle of this intersection, as all those cars were beginning to honk for me to get out of their way, so I hurriedly jumped out of my car, and with the driver's side door hanging open, I began to push and guide the car to the side of this highway, steering with one hand and pushing the car with my other hand, I was moving along very nicely when I suddenly felt something around my ankles, when I looked down, I saw slacks wrapped around my ankles and my white silky panties glistening in the bright sun. I had no other alternative but to pause long enough to pull up my pants, button them up, all the while all these cars stayed put, but still honking like crazy. By the time a couple of guys had put their eyes back into their sockets, I was off the highway, and safely by the side of the road.

Chapter 35

I thought I was being a good wife and mother, I kept everything under control around the house, dinner was on the table, like clockwork, when Miles came home from work, like the good old days, when families still sat around the dinner table and discussed the day's events. One evening, my perfect life took a sudden twist that would upset my applecart. It was a normal evening, the children looking out the window, waiting for daddy, well, daddy wasn't showing up as usual, we waited as long as we could, then finally had dinner without him. I was very concerned of what could have happened to him, fearing an accident, but I had no way to get in touch with him. There were no cellphones at that time, and I waited for a call that never came. The children went to bed and I stayed up waiting til midnight, then he finally came staggering in the door, obviously quite inebriated. I asked the obvious question, "Where have you been?" He said, "I had a few drinks with the boys after work." I let it slide as an unfortunate one time incident. I even had to chuckle a bit as he headed for the bedroom, his long legs wobbling a little like the scarecrow in the Wizard of Oz, but I was glad that he was home safe. "No harm done, yet!" This 'drinking with the boys' soon became a regular routine, coming home very late or maybe not at all. As time went on, the coming years changed everything. Something I was ill prepared to deal with. All my pleading, and maybe even bitching, fell on deaf ears, doing no more than making me the nagging wife now. All the more reason for him to stay away. I got very concerned that he might lose his job, but then how could he, when his boss was one of his best drinking buddies.

One morning, Miles left early for work as he always had, but this time he returned home within a couple of hours experiencing severe chest pains. I immediately rushed him to the hospital where the diagnosis was a heart attack. When the doctor ordered eight weeks of complete bed rest, my mind kicked into overtime. My little sewing business income wouldn't be sufficient anymore, and I could see my 'stay at home mom' days were coming to an end. I wasted no time in checking out the want ads in the newspaper and soon realized that I had very limited skills. There were no sewing factories close by I knew of. All I'd ever done was being a waitress, but that was working nights and weekends when I needed to be home with the children. I knew how to drive a team of mules, but I saw no ads for that. I was facing a blank wall, so for the time being, Annette being in kindergarten for a couple of more months, I took a job at the school cafeteria which would fit the bill for the time being. They hired me right away and I soon realized why; nobody stayed on that job very long. All they had me do was wash cheese graters as big as a car. I stayed until school was over and Miles was back to work. Eunice was now in high school, and became a big help to me when I found a job at a laundry and dry cleaning establishment, conveniently located close to home. I was making $1.44 an hour and I had arranged carpooling for school transportation with friends from church. Eunice was a very responsible help for me tending the children after school. She even became a pretty good cook. Having dinner ready by the time I got home from work. She learned to make a most delicious tuna casserole, on which I complemented her and told her how proud I was of her. After that, we had tuna casserole four nights a week and I haven't made it since! When she turned sixteen years old, her high school was not offering driver's ed, so it became my responsibility to teach her how to drive a car. At that time, the big department stores were still closed on Sundays, so I took advantage of their big empty parking lots where we'd go and spin around in our little Renault, which by now had a coffee can for a muffler. Anyone that didn't see us could surely hear us. Sorry if I disturbed anyone taking a Sunday nap. Although, it was an exciting experience, we laughed together, we cried together, but in the end she became an excellent driver. Marilyn was lucky to get her driver's ed training when she was in high school, where it was offered. My girls were so good about doing everything I asked of them, never a complaint. They are hardworking responsible wives and mothers today, and they are my pride and joy. I'm so proud of all their achievements in life and the way they look out for me in my old age.

To my total surprise, as soon as Miles went back to work, he seemed to pick up right where he left off, staggering in at all hours of the night, sometimes not even coming home at all or even staying away weekends, which now made me very suspicious that this has become something more than just out 'drinking with the boys'! My pleading fell on deaf ears and went nowhere, except to drain my strength, so I simply stopped pleading and used my energy elsewhere and went on with my life. One good thing was, after Walt Disney had opened his first Disneyland Park in Anaheim, very near where we lived, the girls and I would go to this fantasyland as often as possible. It was like walking into another world that you never wanted to leave at the day's end. They were very pleasant outings. Every time we went there, we had loads of fun. My children, my grandchildren, and my great grandchildren that still live in California still go there often, buying season tickets every year. I was getting used to my new routine, now working full time, doing all my housework, and doing a lot of sewing late into the evening after work. I usually went to bed dead tired and slept fitfully, no more staying up waiting for Miles to come home. I had other things to worry about. I liked my job well enough; I was working in the dry cleaning department where I inspected all the clothes before they went out the door. The man that ran this delivery route for the establishment was an older grey haired, somewhat sophisticated looking, married gentleman. He was always anxious to get started on his route. As soon as he came in every morning, I accommodated him and inspected his clothes first, which I wasn't supposed to be doing, but we never told the boss. This fellow was very appreciative and always complemented me on how fast I worked. One day, my boss put me in charge of closing up shop at the end of the day, where everyone went home at five pm, and I had to stay and take care of last minute customers, then I had to lock up at six pm. This one evening I was locking up when I heard someone coming in the back door, which was where the alley was. That door was to be locked at all times, except for the delivery route man, he always had a key because of his hours on the route. I walked to the back to see what I had heard, and I was so relieved that it was just the route man coming in the door. Before I had a chance to say a word, he totally surprised me when he walked up to me wrapping his arms around me and tried to kiss me. I was so caught off guard, I begged him to let me go, but instead he became somewhat forceful, so I went to work with all the strength I had in me. I scratched and I kicked and even screamed, I kneed him in the groin and soon he didn't have his arms around me any longer, because he now needed them to shield himself with. He suddenly let go of me, and quickly disappeared through the back door in which he came. He had a surprised look on his face when I started to fight him, so I got the feeling that he had done this before, maybe with a more willing partner. I had to sit down for a minute to get my wits together, then I locked up and went home. No one at home to talk to, I had a very restless night wondering how I was going to face this animal the next morning. I wondered if I should report this to the boss, but I was afraid I might lose my job. So that morning, I went on to work as usual. This fellow came in and without saying a word, not even looking at me, he grabbed his load and left. He came back in at lunch time, which was his normal routine, and that's when he profusely apologized to me for what he had done. He said to me, "You are quite a lady, your husband should be proud of you!" He then promised never to bother me again. That wasn't good enough for me; I'd already made up my mind to look for another job and kept vigil never to be caught with this man alone again. I was once again scanning the want ads in the newspaper, looking for a job.

One Sunday morning I ran into a stroke of luck, when a lady from church offered me a job, working for a doctor that also happened to be her husband. I was definitely interested, especially when she offered me so much more money than I was making at the dry cleaners. I readily accepted her offer and gave notice to my boss immediately. He was very surprised and asked me why. Here was my chance to tell him my real reason, but instead, I told him that I was offered another job paying substantially more money than I was making. He surprised me when he told me that he would match it if I stayed on. That boosted my moral considerably, and gave me such confidence that I was doing something right. I was really surprised when my co-workers gave me a going away party on my last day at work and gave me a gift of a cross pen and pencil set, an identical gift I had received many years prior, when I won a spelling contest, except, this time I got to keep it. I was very busy making myself a couple of white uniforms, a requirement at my new job. I went through a trauma period, worrying about being qualified working in a doctor's office; Miles was never home evenings to help unload my or cope with all this anxiety and the unknown. The first day on my new job, I walked into a room of mostly Spanish speaking patients, a doctor was Spanish, so all I heard was everyone speaking Spanish, of which I understood not a word. When I was in high school, I took Latin and was now sorry that I didn't take Spanish instead. I gave this new job all I had trying to understand these nice people that needed help, I was continually interrupting this doctor's wife that worked in the office. I knew I was unqualified for this job, and my nerves were coming unglued little by little, till I felt it necessary to tell them that I felt uncomfortable every day for fear that I might make a serious mistake with this language barrier. They were understanding and I agreed to stay on, till they could replace me with a Spanish speaking person, I hope! I was back looking at the want ads in the newspaper once again. This time I began to look into working in a bank, where working hours would fit my schedule, and I loved weekends off working at the doctor's office. I it didn't seem like I had much luck till I saw an ad in the newspaper want ads one morning, that Hughes Aircraft was hiring, I wasn't sure if that would be something that I could do, but I decided to give it a try. I went for an interview that took up most of my day, they were giving me so many tests, oral tests, written tests, and they watched me assemble small parts, as I was being timed. They took me to this huge plush office, with a nicely dressed gentleman sitting behind a huge desk. He asked me some questions, one of which was, "what do you with your hands."? I was caught off guard for a moment, thinking it an odd question and I wasn't sure what to say, so I said, "Well I do housework, I sew, I play piano, I do needlework, crocheting and knitting, and that's about it. Then he told me that I had scored very high on my dexterity test, he asked me to follow him to another room. We entered a fairly small room through a thick, refrigerator like door. All four walls in that room were blackboards covered with written formula's in white chalk, which reminded me a little of my chemistry room in high school. In the center of this room sat, what looked like an incubator you see in baby nurseries in hospitals. It had two sealed rubberized holes on the one side. They asked me to stick both of my hands through these rubberized holes and had me assemble some very small parts to some larger parts, I was very nervous having these guys, in their expensive suits, looking over my shoulder the whole time. When I finished, they led me to another office and handed me instructions to go next door and see their company doctor for a physical exam, but all he did was tap me on the knee with a little hammer, till my foot hit him in the face. Then I was told to return to this nice plush office I had visited earlier, where this same gentleman told me that I had been hired. He proceeded to give me final instructions, telling me that my working hours would be from, 3am to 12pm, from Wednesday to Wednesday,

Monday and Tuesday being my days off. That was bad enough, but when he continued to tell me that I would be required to have a blood test every six months, because of some possible radiation exposure, I began to look for the nearest exit. Consequently, I quit that job an hour after I was hired. It was a sad ride home. After dinner, and the children now in bed, and no one to talk to, I looked into space, and I began to sing, the country tune, that Jim Reeves had just released, with the lyrics that seemed to fit my mood that went like this:

FOUR WALLS TO HEAR ME

FOUR WALLS TO SEE

FOUR WALLS SO NEAR ME

CLOSING IN ON ME.

I then retired for the night. The next morning, it cheered me up to watch my girls cheerfully getting ready for school, not a care in the world, and I decided that I was going to do my best in a situation I didn't seem to have any control over.

The one thing we all looked forward to was the two weeks of summer vacation we spent driving to Rupert to visit my family, who were always ready and waiting for us, where we partied hearty for a solid two weeks. Since we all played piano and accordions, we had dance parties all night. We also had very nice get-togethers whenever any of them came to visit us in California, going to the beautiful beaches, Disneyland, Knott's Berry Farm, and more. We were a very close family, and tried to get together as often as possible.

My marriage was hardly a marriage anymore, so I decided that I needed to get serious about my future and look for a job that might give me some security of my own, just in case. I came up with a couple of options and thought working at a post office would fit my schedule with the children, with holidays off, daytime working hours. I wasted no time going to inquire if or when they were hiring. They had me fill out an application. I took the civil service test, which I passed. They said they would call me, so I waited, but I kept looking at the want ads, but praying for that phone call. Finally, I did get a phone call, but a long shot from the one I was waiting for. This call turned my world upside down and inside out. The call happened to be bad news, telling me that my mother-in-law had suffered a serious heart attack and was rushed to the hospital, so my father-in-law was asking me if I could rush over and open her fabric store.

It was lucky that I happened to be home and had helped her out before in a time of need. So I rushed to Buena Park, in Orange County, which was actually quite a drive. I was soon in my element, patronizing with nice customers that were sewing for their families, as I had been doing for my family. I would come home and have a good night's sleep, I suppose from the therapy of it all. I had almost forgotten about that long awaited phone call from the post office when that call finally came. Now I felt like I'd been caught in a whirlwind. The doctors had already informed my mother-in-law that it was very unlikely that she could ever return to her business, if ever. That's when my father-in-law offered me a deal that was too good to refuse. Making this decision made me feel like I had just downed a fifth of Jack Daniels. I took some time to talk it over with Miles, when and if. His answer to me was, "I wish you would buy the store, because it would make mother very happy". I was hoping he would ask me if it would make me happy too, but he said no more. I took into consideration that this would mean, going into a substantial amount of debt, working very long hours, seven days a week, but I would be doing something I really enjoyed, and the long hours would be to my benefit if I was successful. I had to make a decision, I went for it and soon became the proprietor of my own store. I thought I better be successful, the venison chili was long gone. In hindsight, I think I made the right decision for my sanity at the time, but I'd made the wrong decision, for my future well-being. I look at it this way, what would be the use of having a great retirement, if you have to spend it in a nut house.

My business being based in Buena Park made it necessary for us to sadly lease out our beautiful home in Torrance and make the move to Buena Park, so, in August of 1967 we moved into a three bedroom condo very close to the store and we started life anew! Eunice was in her second year of college at Cal State Fullerton; Marilyn started her sophomore year at Kennedy High School in Buena Park, and Annette was in fourth grade at a public school. The girls were so grown up and were a huge help to me at the store. As a matter of fact, Eunice and Marilyn both became good seamstresses on their own and still do a lot of sewing for their own families. Annette was still a little too young and really never got into this sewing business herself. She was always wanting to party, and she still does have a lot of parties. I also hired a nice lady who was a good seamstress and had a lot of artistic abilities which became a definite asset to my business. It wasn't long before my business had picked up considerably and I felt confident that I probably did make the right decision. My mother-in-law was recuperating nicely by now and she even enjoyed an occasional visit to the store and "yes", she was very happy that I purchased her store, but I was happy too. Her son Boyd, my old boss from the drive-in, in Rupert, was now a successful physician at Hollywood Presbyterian Hospital. He had a nice family of his own and a very nice home where we enjoyed a lot of family get-togethers and reminiscing our drive-in days. When his daughter got married, they had a beautiful wedding for her, followed by a lavish reception. It was there where I was introduced to a glass of the most delicious wine, which was being served in beautiful Waterford crystal stemware. I was so overwhelmed how delicious it was, I enquired about it and learned that it was a brand of Blue Nun. My father liked wine, and he always had red wine around the house, mainly a port wine, but the only wine I ever bought for myself had been a bottle of Mogan David grape wine, which I had developed a taste for at the communion table at church. Needless to say, soon after this experience at that wedding reception, I purchased a bottle of this blue nun wine and at the same time I bought myself a fake crystal wine glass. This spoiled me for life where I almost exclusively want to drink my wine in a nice crystal wine glass. Now I enjoy a nice cold, delicious glass of wine before dinner. My bottle of Valium went into the trash and the Blue Nun in my refrigerator. I felt like I was coming up in the world, learning, experiencing.

One day I received a notice that our renters were moving out, after which I went to look at the house and found that they had left it in complete shambles. Again, I got out the ladder, buckets of paint, and painted the entire house. It looked so nice when I finished that I couldn't bear leasing it again and put it up for sale. It looked like we would be in Buena Park to stay. We sold our house rather quickly and then purchased another house in Buena Park, an older four bedroom house close to where the store was located. It needed a face lift, so out came the ladder and buckets of paint and once again I painted every room throughout this house. I made new curtains and drapes for all the windows, because, I planned to stay put for a very long time. Ha! Ha!

I'm still not sure what my logic was; I had gone from buying a two bedroom house the first time, then to a three bedroom house, and on to a four bedroom house. All the while, the family was shrinking. Eunice had graduated from college and had moved to the valley where she had a good job. Marilyn had gotten married to a very nice Navy man and had moved away to a Navy base where her husband was stationed. Annette was still in high school and very active in school activities. It gave me a lot of pleasure to watch the girls branch out and do remarkably well, but at the same time, it became eerily quiet around the house. Miles was still enjoying his night life away from home, even staying away some weekends and many times he didn't come home for weeks at a time. It was obvious that this had become more than "just out with the boys." I was beginning to see trouble looming on the horizon, but I had this huge obligation of running a business. So I put my heart and soul into my work, thinking, "let the chips fall where they may," and fall they did!

Chapter 36

One morning I got a big surprise, rumors began to circulate about a gigantic fabric store coming to the area, no more than a half mile away, taking over a vacant supermarket building. I became extremely concerned about surviving competition of that nature so close to my own business, and well, I should have been. As soon as they opened their doors, there was an immediate and drastic drop in my business. I went snooping around at this new competition and I was appalled at what I found. They were underselling me by a very big margin and I could well understand losing customers for bargains. I might have done the same thing if I were on the other side of the cutting table. I was mentally and physically devastated. My store lease happened to be coming up for renewal so I had to do some serious soul searching and many sleepless nights before I came up with a final and sad conclusion. With tears streaming down my face, I was soon making "Going out of Business" signs! I ended up being extremely lucky to walk away from my store "debt free" but with a very bruised ego.

Chapter 37

Now I was starting all over again, job hunting. I could have worked in any fabric store anywhere around, but I didn't really want to measure fabric all day for somebody else's customers. So when one of my lady customer friends offered to help me get work, doing market research where she herself worked, I took advantage of the offer for the time being, after taking the required training period I learned that a lot of this work entailed going door to door placing consumer products in people's homes for them to use, then allow us to return at a later date for their evaluation of the product they now had a chance to try. When I was given my first job they gave me a map of my route to deliver a product. My first day, I went to the warehouse as instructed to pick up this product and was taken aback a bit as I watched them load up my car, completely stuffing the trunk of my car, loading up the back seat to the ceiling, packing the front passenger seat until I barely had room to drive, with loaves and loaves of "Weber's Bread." My car was beginning to smell like an oven and I couldn't help but have a brief flashback thinking that I was being haunted, because many years before, the very first slice of "store bought" bread I'd ever had the privilege to eat, happened to be "Weber's Bread!" I didn't think that I would like this job very much, but I was making friends with the ladies I worked with, especially my supervisor, Shirley, whom I stayed close friends with for many years, until she passed away recently. Annette had by now graduated from high school and moved to the valley to work with her sister, so my evenings became long and quiet. Miles was still hanging on to his job during the day and going out most of the nights. Many times the girls at work had asked me to join them for dinner and a movie. I had always turned them down, but one evening, I decided to join them, and found it an extremely enjoyable evening. I began joining them more often and enjoyed this relaxing recreation. When I was offered a supervisor position with the company I was working for I actually stayed for several years doing something I really didn't want to do for the rest of my life, but decided to keep on trucking, then one day I happened to run into an old friend of mine who was now a real estate agent. As we happily chatted along, she popped up and said to me, "Etta, you should try selling real estate; I make a lot of money!" I said, "Did you say you make a lot of money? Where do I start?" She gave me some good advice which was music to my ears. I immediately enrolled in a real estate school which she had recommended. I quit my job and put every ounce if energy I had left studying and cramming for a real estate license that I hoped would very soon be my future, once and for all. "Lots of luck!"

As I was attending the real estate classes, I became determined to prove my professor wrong when he repeatedly told our class that we should expect to flunk the real estate exam the first time we took it, because almost everybody does. I spent all my time studying and cramming. I had a goal and I meant to achieve it. Finally the big day, our final exam. I walked into this big room and saw that there were rows and rows of tables and chairs that had the real estate exam placed on the table in front of each chair. This test looked as thick as a telephone book. After a few instructions, where we were told to take our time, that a lot of people take the biggest part of the day to finish the test, they told us there would be a lunch break. I was fairly calm and fully prepared and anxious to get started. The first thing I did was pray, then I went through this whole book, page by page, and answered each question that I was absolutely sure of, then I thumbed through the second time to answer the questions I was fairly sure of. I went through this process until the last few questions, so I guessed at those and never left one question unanswered. Our instructor had told us that after taking the test, within a week or so, if we received a small postcard in the mail, that would be an indication that we flunked the test, but if we passed the test, we would receive a large brown manila envelope, in the mail. I looked holes through my window, waiting for the mailman every single day. Then one day I saw him stuff a large brown manila envelope into my mailbox, and I nearly ran him over getting to my mail that morning. I was so excited to have passed this test, I immediately ran out and purchased a bottle of Blue Nun, then I drove to the school, walked up to the instructors desk, and said, "Thank you for being such a good instructor!" He had this surprised smile on his face as I walked out.

Chapter 38

Now the tide had turned and I was inundated with
real estate brokers, coming to my door, wanting me
to come work for their company. I thought that I
had truly found the "pot of gold" at the end of the
rainbow. I carefully made my choice and proudly
went to work as a real estate agent, hoping to be
"making a lot of money." The first instruction that
my broker gave me was to tell me that we now
needed to look like real estate agents. He looked at
my car and said it was nice enough, but then he said
I need to carry a nice briefcase. I rushed to the store
and purchased myself a very nice Samsonite
briefcase, which cost me $85, which I had to put it
on my credit charge account, thinking, "no
problem" I would soon pay for it making all this "a
lot of money." That would just pile up in my bank.
My usual luck was, it happened to be the year of
the Carter administration where mortgage rates
soared as high as 21% and real estate was almost at
a standstill. I tried my very best pounding sidewalks,
scouting for business, doing everything my broker
told me to do. I was carrying a beautiful briefcase
with nothing in it. I looked good, but my bank

account didn't. Sometime later, I happened to run into my real estate friend again. I asked her, "Where is this 'a lot of money' I'm supposed to be making?" She replied, "Be patient, it takes time!" I said, "How much time, I'm getting old!" there was not much more I could do but to keep on polishing my car and carrying a fancy empty briefcase. I worked hard for weeks to finally sell my first house, which was somewhat encouraging. One morning, as I was getting ready to go to work, I noticed crow's feet around my eyes. Whoa!!! I thought maybe I should begin to work a little less and play a little more, instead of spending all my evenings feeling sorry for myself. Then and there I made it a point to join the girls more often the next time they asked me out to dinner and a movie. This one evening they called me and wanted to know if I wanted to go dancing at a club in Newport Beach that had a band on weekends. I decided to go and had a most wonderful time dancing the night away, and I didn't notice that those "crow's feet" around my eyes ever got in the way for the lack of dancing partners. We stayed and danced until the place closed down, so I didn't arrive home until after 1 am, and got the surprise of my life, when I walked in and saw Miles sitting on the sofa, drinking a beer and he was very angry. He wanted to know where I had been, I assumed that he must have gotten wind somehow that I was going out that evening. I frankly told him the truth, that I had been out dancing and that I had such a good time and I couldn't wait to go again. Then I added that, what I would really like, was for him to come home from wherever he hung out all the time so we could go dancing together. Well he didn't, and I did! Maybe my daughter was right when she always said, "My mother will take and take and take, but when she's had enough there is nothing left but hair and gristle!"

Chapter 39

My good friend Shirley had been making several trips to Las Vegas, mainly to visit her mother and stepfather, who lived there. Her mother had been very ill with terminal cancer. Sometime after she passed away, I got a call from Shirley asking me if I wanted to join her and two other girls and go to Las Vegas for the weekend. She said that her stepfather had gotten us free rooms at a major hotel and tickets to the Liza Minnelli show. That sounded very inviting and I had never been to Las Vegas, except when we used to drive through there on our way to Idaho every summer. I was somewhat leery but I told her that I would go, only if I could drive my own car. So I did drive there and met them at this hotel casino, where we had very nice rooms. We were all dressed up for the evening when there was a slight tap on the door and in walks this handsome, olive skinned smiling debonair looking gentleman. Shirley introduced him to us as, Joe, her recently widowed stepfather. For a minute he made my heart flutter, but I was really impressed when he held and kissed each of us ladies hands. He got the party going by suggesting that we order up a bottle of wine, waving the wine list, which is always left in the rooms, he asked, "Who knows of a good wine?" He'd hit the nail on the head with me, as I quickly said, "I do!" I looked at the list, deep in prayer by now, that I would find what I was looking for. Then I saw the magic word (Blue Nun). I said to them, "This is a good wine," and they said, "We'll take your word for it" so they ordered it up, Joe uncorked and poured, we all raised our glasses for a toast. Everyone took a sip and almost in unison they said, "This wine is delicious, we didn't know Etta was a wine connoisseur" I took the complement gracefully, but at the same time I was thinking, "How can I be a wine connoisseur when I haven't been any farther than my own backyard?" I did not tell them that I had actually gone from Mogen David grape wine straight to Blue Nun. I knew nothing about any other kinds of wines.

The Liza Minnelli dinner show was spectacular. I was so glad that I had decided to come. Joe hung around with us all weekend. We went dancing and had an unbelievable good time. It was like going to Disneyland, you didn't want to go back home. After that, there were many of those kinds of trips. Joe always being very generous, getting us free rooms, dinners and shows, through some connections he had. I couldn't believe my luck. He always joined us for those evenings and I was beginning to really enjoy being in his company and his carefree happy attitude. Maybe I was even beginning to have feelings for him, which I thought to be dangerous, because in his own words in our conversations, he made it perfectly clear that he was enjoying his new bachelor life and intended to keep it that way. I soon stopped going to Vegas altogether, and put my heart and soul getting my real estate going, but it wasn't going anywhere very fast. It seemed like the more experienced agents were always a step ahead of us greenhorns. I was working hard, long hours, with little or no pay coming in. I found it to be a thankless job. Not much I could do about it, but to keep on trying. Then!!! This one evening I received a phone call that would blow my existing life to the extreme. It was Joe on the line, and he wanted to know why I hadn't been coming to Vegas, and was I planning to come anytime soon?

My whole body began to tingle, almost dropping the telephone as if I was paralyzed. Holding on tight to the telephone, I calmly told him that I had been very busy with my real estate but that I would probably be coming again sometime. I wasted no time calling Shirley to see how soon she'd be going back to Vegas again. So the very next time she went, I went with her. Needless to say, the inevitable transpired. I filed for divorce from Miles. Our house in Buena Park was sold. Assets were evenly divided. I was anxiously looking forward to go on with my new life and I hoped Miles would also. He didn't take very kindly to the divorce, but we remained civil, until he passed away a few years later.

?

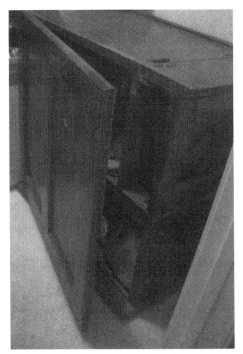

Doctor machine cabinet

Jars inside doctor machine cabinet

Mother making balls of yarn for her loom

Rupert house we moved to from Declo

Our house in North Dakota, 50 years later – notice
extension for the garage

Me and my sidekick, Hildegard

My first car in California, Marilyn in rumble seat

Dad & Mother looking at the Pacific Ocean for the first time

My 8th grade graduation picture

My high school graduation picture

Boyd, M.D., my boss from Cooper's drive-in in Rupert, talking over old times!

Miles & the deer he shot with his bow & arrow

Dad & his accordion

THE FAMILY THAT PLAYS TOGETHER...
SISTERS REUNITE, PERFORM IN RUPERT

Joe and I, The Polka Dots!

Chapter 40

On October 20th, 1979, some two years after I first met Joe, we were married in a Las Vegas chapel with my daughters and family members in attendance.

All my life I had wanted to go to New York, of which I'd heard and read so much about, so that's where we decided to spend our honeymoon. It was an exhilarating experience, to say the least, to see the empire state building, Rockefeller Center, the Statue of Liberty, and much more. But what I didn't like, was riding the subways, especially the day we rode one on our way to Ellis Island to see the Statue of Liberty. As the subway train was loudly clanging along, I saw water trickling down the mossy walls that were flying by. So I asked Joe, "Where is that water coming from?" He said, "Oh, we're travelling under the Hudson River right now!" I screamed, "Under the Hudson River?! Let me out of here!" Passengers were staring at me. But I have to say, all in all, it was a great experience and a trip to remember. We made many more trips after that. We went to Virginia, where all of Joe's family lives, near Washington DC. So I had the opportunity to meet all of them and also got to visit all the historical sites around there, but there was one trip I was now ready to make, that was travelling to North Dakota to visit our old farm, that I had left behind more than 40 years before. The people who had purchased our farm had given all of us an open invitation to come visit any time we wished, even though it was now owned by their son and his family. My parents and siblings had already gone back to visit numerous times, but I never had the desire to until now. So Joe and I travelled there with my brother and his family in their motorhome. We arrived in the small town of Hague and spent our first night there. The ice cream shop was long gone, no ice cream cone that year. The next day, as we were driving through all this open farmland, I was amused to watch Joe staring out the window, when he said, "There really are rock piles out there!" I had told him earlier about some of my farming experiences and I had the understanding that he believed me. The mayor of the little city of Hague happened to be the little neighbor boy way back, who had gone to school with us. He was elated to see us, and looked out for our well-being while we were parked there. We were all having such a good visit sitting in the motorhome, when I popped up with the question, "By the way, Mikey, (his name was Mike) how many children did you have?" He smiled and said, "Sixteen." I chuckled a little and repeated, "How many children did you really have?" With a bigger smile on his face now, he again replied, "Sixteen." Before I could say another word, his wife came walking through the door looking like a model, slender, vibrant and beautiful. I said, "I guess North Dakota has been good to you, Mikey!" The next morning was the big moment. Art decided to first drive us by the little red school house which we had all attended, and was on the way to the farm. When he pulled up to that location, the school was completely gone, all that was left was part of the foundation. I had a feeling of despair as we walked around the grounds. It brought back so many memories and I was soon ready to get away from there. We all piled into the motorhome, then Art couldn't get it started. We were out of gas. We had no cellphones, no way to communicate like we have today. Our only alternative was to sit and wait, hoping someone would come by. Someone finally did come by and were a big help getting us some gas, and we were on our way. I couldn't help but think, "What's new!" There still seems to be a problem coming and going to this school." The feeling and anticipation by now, consumed my whole being, as I watched Art turn onto the same narrow dirt road that still wound through the neighbor's farmland that led to our farm. I nearly stuck my head through the windshield when we came to the top of the little hill and "there it was!" I thought I'd faint, when I saw that it still looked identical to what I had seen when I took that final peek out the rear window of dad's 1938 Ford back in 1941 more than 40 years ago. As we drove up to the yard, we were warmly welcomed by the family living there now, and they showed us all around the farm. The only thing that had really changed, was that they had built a new house on the property, and were now using our little home for storage and a car garage. It was interesting when they told us that its combined living and bedroom was so small, they had to build on an extension in order to fit a car. The windmill was still pumping water as I heard the very familiar sound. Animals were everywhere. I was still somewhat leery to even walk past a chicken for fear it would begin to chase me. All the same old buildings were intact. Then we walked to the barn and I was beginning to think that I even recognized the cows. It seemed like time had stood still all those years.

The nostalgia was becoming more overwhelming and I was beginning to feel a wheezy sensation and I was more than glad when it was time to leave. I did go back to visit this farm, one other time a few years later, when us five sisters named "The Accordion Sisters" were hired to play there at the One Hundredth Centennial Celebration, where a lot of people still remembered us. This time it was an honor and very lucrative trip.

Back from our honeymoon in New York, I had to make a decision whether I should start over and continue doing real estate in the state of Nevada, even though my enthusiasm wasn't there to think about starting all over again. I decided against it and went to work for C.H. Baker shoe company at one of five stores they had in Las Vegas which was the big store that Joe had managed for some 20 years. This store was located in downtown Las Vegas on Fremont Street, right in the middle of all the casino action. It became a very interesting place to work, where tourist customers came from all over the world. I was very surprised one day when a couple that had been my next door neighbors in Torrance, California, many years before, walked in. We had a good chat. There were many more surprises like that, but none that topped the day when this older couple came in to the store. When I asked them the usual question, "Where are you from?" he said, "We are now retired and live in Pocatello, Idaho, but we lived in Rupert for many years when I worked for the railroad there." Bells went off in my head, and I had to ask, "You don't happen to be one of those railroad engineers that always came in for breakfast at Cooper's Drive-In next door?" Somewhat surprised, he said yes, he remembered. When I reminded him that I am that shy red headed green eyed waitress that always waited on them, then I reminded him how they used to enjoy teasing me, relentlessly, just to watch me blush a beet red. He paused a bit, and then he threw his arms up in the air and reached out to hug me. I wasn't sure if I should hug him back, or slap him. An extremely rare incident, to say the least. There was never a dull moment at that store, like the day I had just finished washing and polishing our two large store display windows, when this panhandler walked up and proceeded to aim and piss all over my clean windows. I thought of running to stop him, but soon thought better of it, for fear of getting sprayed myself. It was a blessing when the company opened two new stores at a local mall. They gave Joe their big store to manage and they gave me a manager position for their smaller ladies high end shoe store. It was great for us to be able to work at the same mall and to each have our own stores. Life was good. We went dancing often. We saw spectacular Las Vegas shows, had lovely dinners at some of the finest restaurants. We also travelled to California quite often to visit the children and grandchildren there, we'd go walk in the warm sand along the beautiful beaches. Two of my daughters, Eunice and Annette, had also moved to Las Vegas by then. Marilyn and Dave had too many years invested in their jobs to make the move, but it was nice to be able to visit California. Everything seemed rosy, Then!!

Chapter 41

One unfortunate day at work, I was walking in the mall heading back to my store and with the high heel of my shoe stepped on a plastic price tag and flew through the air like a flying trapeze, landing on the hard marble floor, breaking my right foot and three ribs. I was rushed to the hospital where they put a cast on my foot, and I was laid up for six weeks and finally glad to go back to work. It wasn't long before I developed other health problems. I needed a full hysterectomy. where it was discovered that I had cancer, which put me out of commission longer than I'd like to say. With all the follow up treatments I needed I was very fortunate to come out of that completely cured. I was very happy to go back to work again, walking very carefully on those marble floors, but the klutz that I am, I was climbing a ladder one day, reaching for some shoes on a top shelf, when the ladder gave way and I came tumbling down onto a cement floor. Back to the hospital I went, where they were beginning to know me quite well. The x-ray showed that I had a broken lower lumbar (my back). This became a long and painful ordeal that lasted more than three years, which ultimately led me to retire altogether after ten years with the shoe company. Joe decided to retire six months later, after having been with the company more than thirty years. Having so much leisure time now, we decided to make the drive to Virginia to visit Joe's family. I'm not keen on flying, so driving cross country was quite enjoyable for me. We made a stop in Memphis and visited Elvis Graceland. We also stayed over in Nashville and enjoyed a night at the Grand Old Opry. On our return home, we barely walked into the house when suddenly I experienced excruciating pain in my abdomen. The pain became so severe that Joe rushed me to the emergency room, where I was diagnosed with having a bad case of gall stones. By the next day, I was in the operating room having surgery and I hadn't even unpacked my suitcase yet. I recuperated nicely, and was sent home with a clean bill of health. For now!!! Two years after the surgery, I began experiencing severe chest pains and all the symptoms of an oncoming heart attack. As I followed through with all the necessary tests, I was diagnosed with having some blocked arteries which needed immediate attention. I went for my first procedure at 3pm this one day, an angioplasty, where they insert the balloons to open up the arteries (that was before stents came along). This procedure turned out to be unsuccessful and by 5pm I was rushed to surgery for triple bypass heart surgery. I was in the operating room until 10pm, Joe and my daughters were waiting in the waiting room. I had not had time to have been properly prepared for this kind of surgery, so I was later told, that I was a lucky girl to have come through this as well as I did. It was a very lengthy recuperation period for me, but I came out of it very well. I had had so many major surgeries by now when I was in the shower, I saw so many zig zag scars, I wondered if I got in the way when Zorro slashed his famous Z.

Chapter 42

I was feeling strong and healthy again, when BAM! Joe and I were involved in a serious automobile accident that sent us both to the trauma unit, in an ambulance. We were lucky to walk away with only minor injuries due to the fact that we were both wearing our seatbelts. The accident happened to be the fault of the other party; someone driving a white pickup truck rammed into the driver side of our car and pushed us into a service station nearby. After this accident, I seemed to be traumatized every time I saw a white pickup coming towards us.

So our attorney decided to send me to a psychologist. The psychologist gave me one piece of advice. He said that whenever I see a white pickup truck, I should pretend that my car is completely surrounded with a rubber bumper, which would keep me safe, but all that did, was remind me of some other advice I once got, about a brass ring on the bulls nose that would also keep me safe if I pulled on it when the bull came after me. We both recovered nicely and were back to normal once again. Again we had a lot of time on our hands, so we began to look for something where we could be more active. We ended up going to local nursing and retirement homes, to visit and entertain the residents there. I would play piano and accordion, while Joe would delight the residents by dancing with some of them, even getting them up to do the chicken dance. He would take those in their wheel chairs and wheel them around the floor to the beat of the music, and they were so delighted. They loved all this attention and the good peppy music I played. We soon got so many phone calls from these places that we decided to become a real team and named ourselves, "The Polka Dots." We steadily entertained at these homes for the next five years, entertaining nearly every day. It was as rewarding to us as it was to them. Sadly, the time came for us to slow down and stop altogether. Five years had taken its toll. That finally led to five of us sisters to form our own band and we were called, "The Accordion Sisters." We became quite successful, occasionally playing various gigs, which included some travelling having had a good run while it lasted, but unfortunately, we got a late start and we had to give it up. Because, by then the oldest sister was 86 years old and the rest of us not far behind. But some of us just couldn't put our accordions away altogether. So we would get together whenever possible and play for the sheer enjoyment of it. My sister Betty and I now belong to an accordion club, here in Las Vegas, where a group of accordion players get together as often as possible. Naturally, we never miss the annual "Polka Fest" that is held here at the Orleans Casino every February. There we dance and listen to polka bands from all over the country that play for three straight days, where we dance around the clock, and that won't stop until we drop.

Epilogue

As of today, December 2012, Joe and I still live in the same house we bought, brand new, when we were married more than thirty years ago.

Our precious daughters watch over us and spoil us with such love and kindness; we are more than comfortable and very content. Joe and I are in reasonably good health and working at staying that way. We walk, we swim, and we enjoy our mountain of friends; we still make the drive to California, as often as we can, to visit our daughter Marilyn and son-in-law Dave, plus all the grandchildren who still live in California. We love to go to the beaches there and stomp through the warm sand with our bare feet as the water swirls around them. If we want more excitement, we visit our twelve great grandchildren, for a little while! We plan to keep on going, but, just to stay on the safe side, we did purchase two very comfortable reclining rocking chairs waiting in the wings. They're beginning to look inviting.

Made in the USA
San Bernardino, CA
13 August 2019